BBC ACTIVE

D1142663

GET BY
CHINESE

KAN QIAN
WANG XIAONING
with **KAN JIA**

BBC Active, an imprint of Educational Publishers LLP, part of the Pearson Education Group
Edinburgh Gate, Harlow, Essex, CM20 2JE, England

© Educational Publishers LLP 2008

BBC logo © BBC 1996. BBC and BBC ACTIVE are trademarks of the British Broadcasting
Corporation

First published 2008.

ISBN-13: 978-1-4066-4291-9

Cover concept: Emma Wallace
Cover photograph: Organics image library/Alamy
Insides concept design: Nicolle Thomas
Layout: eMC Design (www.emcdesign.org.uk)
Publisher: Debbie Marshall
Development manager: Tara Dempsey
Senior production controller: Franco Forgione
Marketing: Fiona Griffiths
Audio producer: Martin Williamson, Prolingua Productions
Sound engineer: Studio AVP
Presenters: Amanda Weston, Sarah Wang, Sun Chen

Printed in UK by Ashford Colour Press Ltd.
The Publisher's policy is to use paper manufactured from sustainable forests.

All photographs supplied by Alamy Images.
p7 Dennis Cox; p8 Stock Connection Distribution: p12 mediacolor's; p16 Felix Stensson;
p23 The Photolibrary Wales; p30 Jon Arnold Images Ltd; p32 Liu Xiaoyang; p33 Mike
Goldwater; p33 dbimages; p38 PCL; p39 Gordon Sinclair; p41 Dennis Cox; p53
mediacolor's; p57 John Henshall; p61 PCL; p69 JTB Photo Communications, Inc.; p72
Hemis; p74 AM Corporation; p77 Malcolm Park; p83 Michael Soo; p89 View Stock; p90
Sergiu Turcanu; p91 natsukashi; p93 Steve Bloom Images; p101 Ozimages; p107 Kevin
Foy; p111 Keren Su/China Span; p112 Keren Su/China Span; p116 Michael Matthews;
p119 Jon Arnold Images Ltd; p124 Jon Arnold Images Ltd; p125 imagebroker

Contents

Get By in Chinese is divided into colour-coded topics to help you find what you need quickly. Each unit contains practical travel tips to help you get around and understand the country, and a phrasemaker, to help you say what you need to and understand what you hear.

As well as listing key phrases, **Get By in Chinese** aims to help you understand how the language works so that you can build your own phrases and start to communicate independently. The check out dialogues within each section show the language in action, and the try it out activities give you an opportunity to practise for yourself. The link-up sections pick out the key structures and give helpful notes about their use. A summary of all the basic grammar can be found in the Language Builder, pp128-136.

If you've bought the pack with the audio CD, you'll be able to listen to a selection of the most important phrases and check out dialogues, as well as all the as if you were there activities. You can use the book on its own – but the CD will help you to improve your pronunciation.

sounds Chinese

The sound system described here is the modern standard form of spoken Chinese, known as Mandarin Chinese. In Chinese it is called *putonghua*, literally 'common speech'. The written form of the Chinese language has no correlation with its spoken form. A transliteration system using Latin scripts was adopted, called *pinyin*.

The majority of Chinese words are made up of one or two syllables. Sounds that appear before vowels are called 'initials' (like consonants in English) and the remaining sounds are called 'finals'. Each syllable is represented by a Chinese character.

When *ü* follows *j*, *q*, *x* and *y*, it is written as *u*, but still pronounced as *ü* because *u* never occurs after these initials, eg *ju* and *qu*, not *jü* and *qü*.

The apostrophe (') is used to separate two syllables whenever there may be confusion over the syllable boundary. For example, in *shi'er* 'twelve', *shi* and *er* are separate syllables. When *er* comes after another syllable the *e* is dropped, eg *zhe er* becomes *zher*.

Initials	approx English equivalent
b, d, f, g, k, l, m, n, p, s, t, w, y	similar to English
g	like 'g' in 'girl'
h	like 'h' in 'hole' (but with a little friction in the throat)
j	like 'j' in jeep (with the tongue nearer the teeth)
q	a bit like 'ch' in 'cheese' (with the tongue further forward)
z	like 'ds' in 'loads'
c	like 'ts' in 'toasts'
r	a bit like 'r' in 'run' (but with the tongue rolled)
zh	like 'j' in 'jail' (with the tongue further back)
ch	a bit like 'ch' in 'chair' (with the mouth in a round shape)
sh	like 'sh' in 'short'
x	a bit like 'sh' in 'sheep' (the tongue is behind the teeth)

Finals		Finals	
a	like 'a' in 'father'	iang	like 'young'
ai	like 'igh' in 'high' but with a narrower mouth shape	ing	like 'ing' in 'outing'
ao	like 'ow' in 'how'	iong	combine i with ong
an	like 'an' in 'ban'	o	like 'ore' in 'more'
ang	like 'on' in 'monster'	ou	like 'oa' in 'toast'
e	like 'ur' in 'fur' (when e follows 'y', it is like 'e' in 'yes')	ong	like 'ong' in 'long'
		u	like 'oo' in 'boot'
ei	like 'ay' in 'bay'	ua	combine u with a
en	like 'en' in 'tent'	uo	like 'war'
eng	en plus a strong nasal sound, like 'un' in 'hungry'	uai	combine u with ai
		ui	like 'wai' in 'wait'
er	like 'ur' in 'fur' plus 'l'	uan	like 'one'
i	like 'ea' in 'tea'	un	like 'won' in 'wonder'
ia	combine i and a	uang	like 'wan' in 'want'
iao	like 'eow' in 'meow'	ü	like 'oo'
ie	like 'ye' in 'yes'	üe	combine ü with a short ei
iu	like 'you'	üan	combine ü with a short an
ian	like 'yen'	ün	like 'une' in 'tune'
in	like 'in' in 'bin'		

tones and tone changes

One unique feature of the Chinese language is its tones. Every syllable in isolation is given a specific tone which helps to distinguish the meaning. In *putonghua* (Mandarin Chinese) there are four basic tones:

tone mark		
¯	(high-level)	first tone
´	(rising)	second tone
ˇ	(falling-rising)	third tone
`	(falling)	fourth tone

In addition there is a neutral tone. Syllables with neutral tones are pronounced very weakly and are not marked. For example:

妈 *mā*	麻 *má*	马 *mǎ*	骂 *mà*	吗 *ma*
mother	linen	horse	to swear	question word

There are also many characters which share the same pronunciation and same tones but have different meanngs. For example:

梨 *lí*	离 *lí*	笑 *xiào*	孝 *xiào*
pear	to depart	to laugh	filial piety

Tones do change in spoken Chinese. The two most common changes are:

i) When two third tones are together in the same meaning group, the first third tone usually changes to the second tone, eg
    nǐ, hǎo → *ní hǎo* 'hello'

ii) When *bù* (not) is followed by another fourth tone, it changes to the second tone, eg *bú shì* 'no'

In this book, all the *pinyin* words are marked with tones as if each syllable were in isolation. The only exception is *bù* 'not'. It is always marked with the second tone when followed by a fourth tone, eg *bú shì* 'no'.

Bare **Necessities**

etiquette

China is very much a gift-giving society. Do bring a present to your Chinese host or hostess. Do not give Chinese people clocks as present as the expression 'giving you a clock' sounds the same as 'sending you to grave'.

Do not give Chinese people presents with the number four written on them, as in Chinese the word for the number four sounds very similar to the word that means death or to die.

It is acceptable to sneeze or burp in public, but it is considered rude to blow your nose.

names

Chinese surnames come first, followed by given names.
It is normal to call a Chinese person by his or her full name.
If you wish to use a title such as Mr 先生 (*xiānsheng*) or Miss 小姐 (*xiǎojie*), put the title after the surname.

currency

The formal name for Chinese currency is 人民币 (*rénmínbì*), meaning people's currency, and it is abbreviated as RMB with the sign ￥.

In Chinese currency, there are three units: 元 (*yuán*), 角 (*jiǎo*) and 分 (*fēn*). The informal terms are: 块 (*kuài*), 毛 (*máo*). 分 (*fēn*) remains the same. Each unit contains 10 units of the next level down.

So, 1 yuan contains 10 jiao, and 1 jiao contains 10 fen. If you see this price: ￥ 7.63, it is read 七元六角三分 (*qī yuán liù jiǎo sān fēn*) or 七块六毛三分 (*qī kuài liù máo sān fēn*). Very often, the last unit 分 (*fēn*) can be omitted.

greetings
you may say ...

Good morning.	早上好。	*zǎoshang hǎo*
Good evening.	晚上好。	*wǎnshang hǎo*
Good night.	晚安。	*wǎn'ān*
Hello!	你好。	*nǐ hǎo*
How are you?	你好吗?	*nǐ hǎo ma*
Fine, and you?	我很好，你呢?	*wǒ hěn hǎo, nǐ ne*
Goodbye.	再见。	*zàijiàn*
See you later.	一会儿见。	*yī huìr jiàn*
See you tomorrow.	明天见。	*míngtiān jiàn*

useful words and phrases
you may say ...

Excuse me! (to attract attention)	对不起; 劳驾	*duìbuqǐ; láojià*
I'm sorry.	对不起。	*duìbuqǐ*
It doesn't matter./ It's all right.	没关系。	*méi guānxi*
please	请。	*qǐng*
Thank you.	谢谢	*xièxie*
Thank you (very much).	非常感谢。	*fēicháng gǎnxiè*
You're welcome.	不客气。	*bú kèqi*
yes	是的	*shìde*
no	不是	*bú shì*
yes you can	可以	*kěyǐ*
okay	好的	*hǎode*
Of course!	当然 !	*dāngrán*

Bare **Necessities**

English	中文	Pinyin
Are there any ... toilets?	有 ... 吗? 卫生间; 厕所	*yŏu ... ma* *wèishēngjiān; cèsuŏ*
Where is/are ... the town centre?	... 在哪儿? 市中心	*... zài nǎr* *shì zhōngxīn*

Do you have any ...
  change ?
  maps of Beijing?
	有 ... 吗?
	零钱
	北京地图
		yŏu ... ma
		língqián
		bĕijīng dìtú

How much is it?	多少钱?	*duō shǎo qián*
I'd like ... a map.	我想要 ... 。 一张地图。	*wŏ xiǎng yào ...* *yī zhāng dìtú*

I'd like to have
some ...
  coffee.
  tea.
	我想喝点儿 ...。
	
	咖啡
	茶
		wŏ xiǎng hē diǎnr ...
		
		kāfēi
		chá

you may hear ...

中文	Pinyin	English

在 ...
  二层
	zài ...
	èr céng
		It's ...
		  on the first floor.

一直走。	*yìzhí zŏu*	Straight on.
还要别的吗?	*hái yào biéde ma*	Anything else?
对不起,我没有零钱。	*duìbuqĭ, wŏ méi yŏu líng qián*	Sorry, I haven't got any change.
一共二十二块。	*yīgòng èrshí'èr kuài*	22 kuai altogether.

getting things straight
you may say ...

English	中文	Pinyin
Pardon?	再说一遍,好吗?	*zài shuō yī biàn, hǎo ma*

... please.
  Say that again,
  Write it down,
  Speak more slowly,
	请 ...。
	再说一遍
	写下来
	说慢一点儿
		qĭng ...
		zài shuō yī biàn
		xiĕ xiàlái
		shuō màn yī diǎnr

I understand.	我懂了。	*wŏ dŏng le*
I don't understand.	我不懂。	*wŏ bù dŏng*
Do you speak English?	你说英语吗?	*nĭ shuō yīngyŭ ma*
I don't know.	我不知道。	*wŏ bù zhīdào*

talking about yourself

you may say ...

My name is ...	我叫 ...	*wǒ jiào ...*
I'm ...	我是 ... 。	*wǒ shì ...*
British.	英国人	*yīngguórén*
American.	美国人	*měiguórén*
I come from ...	我从 ...来。	*wǒ cóng ... lái.*
London.	伦敦	*lúndūn*
Ireland.	爱尔兰	*ài'ěrlán*
I'm 28 (years old).	我二十八岁。	*wǒ èrshíbā suì*
I'm ...	我 ...。	*wǒ ...*
single.	单身一人	*dānshēn yī rén*
married.	结婚了	*jiéhūn le*
divorced.	离婚了	*líhūn le*
a widow/widower.	爱人去世了	*ài'ren qùshì le*
I have ...	我有 ...	*wǒ yǒu*
two children.	两个孩子。	*liǎng ge háizi*
boy	男孩儿	*nánháir*
girl	女孩儿	*nǚháir*
I'm a ...	我是 ...。	*wǒ shì ...*
student.	学生	*xuéshēng*
lawyer.	律师	*lǜshī*
teacher.	教师	*jiàoshī*
nurse.	护士	*hùshi*
I work in ...	我在 ... 工作。	*wǒ zài ... gōngzuò*
an office.	一间办公室	*yī jiān bàngōngshì*
a shop.	一家商店	*yī jiā shāngdiàn*
I'm on holiday.	我在度假。	*wǒ zài dùjià*
I'm here on business.	我来这儿出差。	*wǒ lái zhèr chūchāi*
I can speak a little Chinese.	我会说一点儿中文。	*wǒ huì shuō yīdiǎnr zhōngwén*

Bare **Necessities**

你会说中文吗?	*nǐ huì shuō zhōngwén ma*	Can you speak Chinese?
你叫什么?	*nǐ jiào shénme*	What's your name?
请允许我介绍一下...	*qǐng yǔnxǔ wǒ jièshào yīxià ...*	May I introduce ...
我的妻子	*wǒde qīzi*	my wife.
我的丈夫	*wǒde zhàngfu*	my husband.
我的同伴	*wǒde tóngbàn*	my partner.
这是 ...	*zhè shì ...*	This is ...
我的男朋友	*wǒde nán péngyou*	my boyfriend
我的女朋友	*wǒde nǚ péngyou*	my girlfriend
很高兴见到你。	*hěn gāoxìng jiàndào nǐ*	Pleased to meet you.
你是哪国人?	*nǐ shì nǎ guó rén*	Which country are you from?
你从哪儿来?	*nǐ cóng nǎr lái*	Where do you come from?
你是做什么的?	*nǐ shì zuò shénme de*	What do you do (for a living)?
你正在休假吗?	*nǐ zhèngzài xiūjià ma*	Are you on holiday?
你结婚了吗?	*nǐ jiéhūn le ma*	Are you married?
你多大了?	*nǐ duō dà le*	How old are you?
你有孩子吗?	*nǐ yǒu háizi ma*	Do you have children?

countries & nationalities

Australia: Australian	澳大利亚: 澳大利亚人	*àodàlìyà: àodàlìyàrén*
Britain: British	英国: 英国人	*yīngguó: yīngguórén*
Canada: Canadian	加拿大: 加拿大人	*jiānádà: jiānádàrén*
China: Chinese	中国: 中国人	*zhōngguó: zhōngguórén*
England: English	英格兰: 英格兰人	*yīnggélán: yīnggélánrén*
France: French	法国: 法国人	*fǎguó: fǎguórén*
Germany: German	德国: 德国人	*déguó: déguórén*
Holland: Dutch	荷兰: 荷兰人	*hélán: hélánrén*
India: Indian	印度: 印度人	*yìndù: yìndùrén*
Ireland: Irish	爱尔兰: 爱尔兰人	*ài'ěrlán: ài'ěrlánrén*
Italy: Italian	意大利: 意大利人	*yìdàlì: yìdàlìrén*
Japan: Japanese	日本: 日本人	*rìběn: rìběnrén*

Korea: Korean	朝鲜: 朝鲜人	*cháoxiǎn: cháoxiānrén*
South Korea: South Korea	国韩: 国韩人	*hánguó : hánguórén*
Malaysia: Malaysian	马来西亚: 马来西亚人	*mǎláixīyà: mǎláixīyàrén*
New Zealand: New Zealander	新西兰: 新西兰人	*xīnxīlán: xīnxīlánrén*
Northern Ireland: Northern Irish	北爱尔兰: 北爱尔兰人	*běiài'ěrlán: běiài'ěrlánrén*
Scotland: Scottish	苏格兰: 苏格兰人	*sūgélán: sūgélánrén*
South Africa: South African	南非: 南非人	*nánfēi: nánfēirén*
Spain: Spanish	西班牙: 西班牙人	*xībānyá: xībānyárén*
United States: American	美国: 美国人	*měiguó: měiguórén*
Wales: Welsh	威尔士: 威尔士人	*wēi'ěrshì: wēi'ěrshìrén*

check out 1

Your colleague is chatting to the taxi driver.

○ 你从哪儿来?
  nǐ cóng nǎr lái

– 我从伦敦来，我是英国人。
  wǒ cóng lúndūn lái, wǒ shì yīngguórén

○ 你有孩子吗?
  nǐ yǒu háizi ma

– 我有两个孩子。
  wǒ yǒu liǎng ge háizi

Q Where is your colleague from?
Does she have any children?

Bare **Necessities**

numbers

0	零	*líng*
1	一	*yī*
2	二	*èr*
3	三	*sān*
4	四	*sì*
5	五	*wǔ*
6	六	*liù*
7	七	*qī*
8	八	*bā*
9	九	*jiǔ*
10	十	*shí*
11	十一	*shíyī*
12...	十二...	*shí'èr...*
20	二十	*èrshí*
21	二十一	*èrshíyī*
22...	二十二...	*èrshí'èr...*
30	三十	*sānshí*
31	三十一	*sānshíyī*
32...	三十二...	*sānshí'èr...*
40	四十	*sìshí*
50	五十	*wǔshí*
99	九十九	*jiǔshíjiǔ*
100	一百	*yī bǎi*
101	一百零一	*yī bǎi líng yī*
102...	一百零二...	*yī bǎi líng èr...*
110	一百一十	*yī bǎi yīshí*
111	一百一十一	*yī bǎi yīshíyī*
112	一百一十二	*yī bǎi yīshí'èr*
113...	一百一十三...	*yī bǎi yīshísān...*
120	一百二十	*yī bǎi èrshí*
121...	一百二十一...	*yī bǎi èrshíyī...*
200	二百	*èr bǎi*
250	二百五	*èr bǎi wǔ*
300...	三百...	*sān bǎi...*
1,000	一千	*yī qiān*
2,000	两千	*liǎng qiān*

3,000...	三千...	*sān qiān...*
10,000	一万	*yī wàn*
100,000	十万	*shí wàn*
one million	一百万	*yī bǎi wàn*
one and a half million	一百五十万	*yī bǎi wǔshí wàn*

There are two sets of Chinese script for numbers, each with the same pronunciation. For example, 1 is represented by both 一 (*yī*) and 壹 (*yī*). One set is for general use, and the other set with more complex characters is used for banknotes and receipts.

	general	banknotes and receipts	
0	零	零	*líng*
1	一	壹	*yī*
2	二	贰	*èr*
3	三	三	*sān*
4	四	肆	*sì*
5	五	伍	*wǔ*
6	六	陆	*liù*
7	七	柒	*qī*
8	八	捌	*bā*
9	九	玖	*jiǔ*
10	十	拾	*shí*

ordinal numbers

1st	第一	*dì yī*
2nd	第二	*dì èr*
3rd	第三	*dì sān*
4th	第四	*dì sì*
5th	第五	*dì wǔ*
6th	第六	*dì liù*
7th	第七	*dì qī*
8th	第八	*dì bā*
9th	第九	*dì jiǔ*
10th	第十	*dì shí*

Bare **Necessities**

changing money

you may say ...

I'd like to change 100 pounds into yuan.	我想换一百英镑的人民币。	*wǒ xiǎng huàn yī bǎi yīngbàng de rénmínbì*
What is the exchange rate?	兑换率是多少？	*duìhuàn lǜ shì duō shǎo*
How much is the commission?	手续费是多少？	*shǒuxù fèi shì duō shǎo*
Do you change traveller's cheques?	可以兑换旅行支票吗？	*kěyǐ duìhuàn lǚxing zhīpiào ma*

you may hear ...

看一下你的护照，可以吗？	*kàn yīxià nǐde hùzhào, kěyǐ ma*	May I see your passport?
手续费是 ...	*shǒuxù fèi shì ...*	The commission charge is ...
一英镑换 ... 元	*yī yīngbàng huàn ... yuán*	The pound is at ... yuan.
一张一百元纸币	*yī zhāng yī bǎi yuán zhǐbì*	a 100 yuan note
一枚一元硬币	*yī méi yī yuán yìngbì*	a 1 yuan coin

check out 2

You're buying a map from a newspaper stand.

○ 对不起，有北京地图吗？
duìbuqǐ, yǒu běijīng dìtú ma

– 有。
yǒu.

○ 多少张？
duō shǎo qián

– 六块八毛。
liù kuài bā máo

> How much is it for a map of Beijing?
> **Q**
> **a)** 8 kuai 6 mao
> **b)** 6 kuai 8 mao
> **c)** 68 kuai

the time

What time is it?	几点了?	*jǐ diǎn le*
What time does the bank …	银行几点 … ?	*yínháng jǐ diǎn …*
open?	开门	*kāimén*
close ?	关门	*guānmén*

you may hear …

上午九点。	*shàngwǔ jiǔ diǎn*	9am
晚上九点。	*wǎnshang jiǔ diǎn*	9pm
现在是下午两点。	*xiànzài shì xiàwǔ liǎng diǎn*	It's 2pm.
早上	*zǎoshang*	in the morning
晚上	*wǎnshang*	in the evening
今天下午	*jīntiān xiàwǔ*	this afternoon
今天	*jīntiān*	today
昨天	*zuótiān*	yesterday
明天	*míngtiān*	tomorrow
现在是两点 … 。	*xiànzài shì liǎng diǎn …*	It's … past two.
十分	*shí fēn*	ten
一刻	*yī kè*	quarter
半	*bàn*	half
中午	*zhōngwǔ*	at noon
半夜	*bànyè*	at midnight
从六点开始	*cóng liù diǎn kāishǐ*	from six o'clock
… 后	*… hòu*	in …
五分钟	*wǔ fēnzhōng*	five minutes
三小时	*sān xiǎoshí*	three hours

Bare **Necessities**

days

Monday	星期一	*xīngqīyī*
Tuesday	星期二	*xīngqī'èr*
Wednesday	星期三	*xīngqīsān*
Thursday	星期四	*xīngqīsì*
Friday	星期五	*xīngqīwǔ*
Saturday	星期六	*xīngqīliù*
Sunday	星期天; 星期日	*xīngqītiān; xīngqīrì*

months

January	一月	*yīyuè*
February	二月	*èryuè*
March	三月	*sānyuè*
April	四月	*sìyuè*
May	五月	*wǔyuè*
June	六月	*liùyuè*
July	七月	*qīyuè*
August	八月	*bāyuè*
September	九月	*jiǔyuè*
October	十月	*shíyuè*
November	十一月	*shíyīyuè*
December	十二月	*shí'èryuè*

check out 3

You're at the bank to get some yuan.

○ 我想换一百英镑的人民币。
wǒ xiǎng huàn yī bǎi yīngbàng de rénmínbì

– 看一下你的护照，可以吗?
kàn yīxià nǐde hùzhào, kěyǐ ma

○ 可以。今天的兑换率是多少?
kěyǐ. jīntiān de duìhuàn lǜ shì duōshǎo

– 一英镑换十五块三毛。
yī yīngbàng huàn shíwǔ kuài sān máo.

Q How much money do you want to change?
What is the exchange rate today?

17

sound check

The initial *j* is pronounced like 'j' in 'jeep' (but with the tongue nearer the lower teeth).

再见	*zàijiàn*	goodbye
休假	*xiūjià*	on holiday

Practise *j* with these words:

加拿大	*jiā'nádà*	Canada
九	*jiǔ*	nine
几点	*jǐ diǎn*	What time is it?
劳驾	*láojià*	excuse me

tone changes

When two third tones are spoken together the first third tone usually changes to a second tone. But it is still written with a third tone:

你好	*nǐ, hǎo* → *ní hǎo*	hello

Practise the change of tone from the third to the second:

两点	*liǎng diǎn*	two o'clock
几点	*jǐ diǎn*	what time?

(See p6 for tones and tone changes)

try it out

know-how

What do you say if you ...

1 wish someone good night, and say you'll see them tomorrow?

2 tell someone you're Scottish, from Edinburgh?

3 tell someone you're 38?

Bare **Necessities**

a 我是苏格兰人，来自爱丁堡。
  wǒ shì sūgélán rén, láizì àidīngbǎo

b 我三十八岁。
  wǒ sānshíbā suì

c 晚安。明天见。
  wǎn'ān. míngtiān jiàn

time flies ...

Match the times to the clocks.

1
2
3
4
5

a 五点半　*wǔ diǎn bàn*
b 十二点十五分　*shí'èr diǎn shíwǔ fēn*
c 两点十分　*liǎng diǎn shí fēn*
d 六点二十分　*liù diǎn èrshí fēn*
e 八点四十分　*bā diǎn sìshí fēn*

as if you were there

You're having a conversation on a train. Follow the prompts:

你好！你说中文吗？
nǐ hǎo! nǐ shuō zhōngwén ma
(Say a little. Then ask where she comes from)
我从西安来。你是英国人吗？
wǒ cóng xī'ān lái. nǐ shì yīngguórén ma
(Ask her to speak more slowly)
我从西安来。你是英国人吗？
wǒ cóng xī'ān lái. nǐ shì yīngguórén ma
(Say no, then say you're American)

linkup

我叫...	*wǒ jiào...*	**My name is** ...
我是英国人	*wǒ shì yīngguó rén*	**I'm** British.
你有孩子吗?	*nǐ yǒu háizi ma*	**Do you have** any children?
我有两个孩子。	*wǒ yǒu liǎng ge háizi*	**I have** two children.
有卫生间吗?	*yǒu wèishēngjiān ma*	**Are there** any toilets?
我想喝点儿咖啡。	*wǒ xiǎng hē diǎnr kāfēi*	**I'd like** to have some coffee.

measure words

In English, we sometimes use 'measure words' to modify certain nouns, for example 'piece' in 'a piece of cake' or 'pair' in 'a pair of trousers'. In Chinese, every noun, when preceded by a number, or 'this' and 'that', must have a measure word inserted before it. Different measure words are used with different nouns:

条 *tiáo* **and** 张 *zhāng*
三条围巾 *sān tiáo wéijīn* three scarves
一张地图 *yī zhāng dìtú* one map

The most commonly used measure word is 个 *ge*:

一个男孩儿 *yī ge nánháir* **one boy**

For more on measure words, see the Language Builder, p128. ·····▷

Bare **Necessities**

number two

二 *èr* and 两 *liǎng* both mean 'two'. 二 *èr* is used in counting and saying other numbers such as 'twenty-two', while 两 *liǎng* is used for telling the time and normally used to quantify things such as 'two books', 'two days', 'two hours':

二十二	*èrshi'**èr***	twenty-two
两个孩子	*liǎng ge háizi*	two children
两点	*liǎng diǎn*	two o'clock
两本书	*liǎng běn shū*	two books

yes/no questions

To ask a yes or no question just add 吗 *ma* to the end of a sentence:

| 他是英国人。 | *tā shì yīngguórén* | He is British. |
| 他是英国人吗? | *tā shì yīngguórén ma* | Is he British? |

saying yes and no

Generally speaking, 是的 *shìde* means yes, and 不是 *bú shì* means no. But they are not used as extensively as in English. They are normally used to answer questions that contain the verb 是 *shì*:

| 他是英国人吗? | *tā shì yīngguórén ma* | Is he British? |
| 是的/不是 | *shìde/bú shì* | Yes./No. |

For more on yes/no questions, see the Language Builder, p134. ┈┈┈┈┅>

Getting **Around**

arriving by air

International flights from most countries arrive at either Beijing Capital Airport, or Shanghai Pudong Airport. You can then catch internal flights to most Chinese cities.

All airports throughout China offer shuttle bus services to the downtown area, either to the CAAC (the Civil Aviation Administration of China) office, or similar downtown location. At Shanghai Pudong Airport, you can catch the Maglev 磁悬浮 (*cíxuánfú*), a kind of bullet train which only takes ten minutes to get to the city centre.

by train

All passenger trains in China are numbered with a roman letter in front of the number to indicate the category of the train. The main types include: P-category (ordinary trains) 普通列车 (*pǔtōng lièchē*), K-category (fast ordinary trains) 普快列车 (*pǔkuài lièchē*), T-category (express fast trains) 特快列车 (*tèkuài lièchē*), Z-category (express non-stop) 直达特快 (*zhídá tèkuài*), D-category (high-speed trains) 动力车组 (*dònglì chēzǔ*). On most long distance trains, there are three ticket choices: 软卧 (*ruǎn wò*) soft-sleepers, 硬卧 (*yìng wò*) hard-sleepers or 硬坐 (*yìng zuò*) hard-seats.

Each soft-sleeper compartment contains four small berths (like two sets of bunk beds). Soft-sleepers are the most comfortable and are the most expensive. Hard-sleeper berths, are divided into upper, middle and lower berths.

car hire

Car hire is becoming popular. In China, people drive on the right side of the road. Even when the traffic light is red, traffic can still turn right. The speed limit in the city is between 30 and 50 kilometres per hour, and between 80 and 100 kilometres on the motorway. On most motorways, there are manned toll gates.

taxi

Taxis are a convenient and inexpensive means of transportation in various cities in China. The English word taxi is on top of all taxis in major cities. Simply raise your hand to hail a taxi. Before you get into a taxi. check if there is a meter and make sure that the driver has a business permit.

The business permit is usually displayed inside the car with the driver's name, driving license number, and the company the driver works for. If you need a car for more than four passengers, you need to book a minibus.

by bus

Buses can be quite crowded, especially during the rush hour. One of the methods used to solve the rush hour problem is to divide buses on the same route into fast buses and slow buses. Fast buses stop at few selected stops, which are sometimes announced when the bus gets to the stop, and slow buses stop at every stop.

Most buses have an attendant who sells tickets. When there isn't a ticket attendant, all you need to do is to throw a one-yuan coin into a coin machine next to the driver. You will need the exact change.

subway

There are subway systems in four Chinese cities: Beijing, Shanghai, Guangzhou and Tianjin. You can buy a ticket for the journey or a kind of pay-as-you-go card. The sign for subway is always written in both Chinese characters and English.

asking the way
you may say ...

Excuse me!	对不起; 劳驾	*duìbuqǐ; láo jià*
May I ask ...?	请问 ...	*qǐng wèn ...*
Where is ...	... 在哪儿?	*... zài nǎr*
the supermarket?	超市	*chāoshì*
the bank?	银行	*yínháng*
the railway station?	火车站	*huǒchē zhàn*
How do I get to ...	去 ... 怎么走?	*qù ... zěnme zǒu*
Tian'anmen Square?	天安门	*tiān'ānmén*
the post office?	邮局	*yóujú*
Is it far?	远吗?	*yuǎn ma*
Is/Are there ... near here?	附近有 ... 吗?	*fùjìn yǒu ... ma*
a cashpoint	提款机; 取款机	*tíkuǎnjī; qǔkuǎnjī*
a park	公园	*gōngyuán*
toilets	卫生间; 厕所	*wèishēngjiān; cèsuǒ*
a taxi rank	出租车站	*chūzūchē zhàn*
Is this the right way to ...	这是去 ... 的路吗?	*zhè shì qù ... de lù ma*
the museum?	博物馆	*bówùguǎn*
the airport?	机场	*jīchǎng*
I'm looking for ...	我在找 ...	*wǒ zài zhǎo ...*
the bus/coach station.	公交车站/长途汽车站	*gōngjiāochē zhàn/ chángtú qìchē zhàn*
the way to the Olympic Village.	去奥运村的路	*qù àoyùn cūn de lù*
an Internet café.	网吧	*wǎng bā*
Where's the nearest ...	离这儿最近的 ... 在哪儿?	*lí zhèr zuìjìn de ... zài nǎr*
petrol station?	加油站	*jiāyóu zhàn*
I'm lost.	我迷路了。	*wǒ mílù le*

Getting **Around**

you may hear ...

那就是。	*nà jiù shì*	There it is!
往 ... 拐。	*wǎng ... guǎi*	Turn ...
右	*yòu*	right.
左	*zuǒ*	left.
在红绿灯。	*zài hónglǜ dēng*	It's at the traffic lights.
在 ... 边。	*zài ... biān*	It's on the ...
右	*yòu*	right.
在 ... 。	*zài ...*	It's to the ...
东边	*dōngbiān*	east.
南边	*nánbiān*	south.
西边	*xībiān*	west.
北边	*běibiān*	north.
走过 ...	*zǒu guò ...*	Cross the ...
这条街。	*zhè tiáo jiē*	street.
这个广场。	*zhè ge guǎngchǎng*	square.
这座桥。	*zhè zuò qiáo*	bridge.
一直走	*yīzhí zǒu*	(keep going) straight on
走 ...	*zǒu ...*	Take ...
右边的第一条街	*yòubiān de dì yī tiáo jiē*	the first street on the right.
左边的第二条街	*zuǒbiān de dì èr tiáo jiē*	the second street on the left.
离这儿(大约)一百米。	*lí zhèr (dàyuē) yī bǎi mǐ*	It's (about) 100 metres away.
在这条路的尽头。	*zài zhè tiáo lù de jìntóu*	It's at the end of the street.
在拐角处。	*zài guǎijiǎochù*	It's on the corner.
在 ...	*zài ...*	It's ...
附近	*fùjìn*	(quite) near
很远	*hěn yuǎn*	far
对面	*duìmiàn*	opposite
前面	*qiánmiàn*	in front of
后面	*hòumiàn*	behind
旁边	*pángbiān*	next to

(See p94 for a list of places you may want to visit.)

check out 1

You stop a passer-by to ask for directions to the post office.

○ 请问，离这儿最近的邮局在哪儿？
   qǐng wèn, lí zhèr zuìjìn de yóujú zài nǎr

– 一直走，在红绿灯往右拐。
   yīzhí zǒu, zài hónglù dēng wǎng yòu guǎi

Q You are told to turn left at the traffic lights: true or false?

hiring a car or bike
you may say ...

I'd like to hire ...	我想租 ...	*wǒ xiǎng zū ...*
a car.	一辆车	*yī liàng chē*
a motorbike.	一辆摩托车	*yī liàng mótuōchē*
a bicycle.	一辆自行车	*yī liàng zìxíngchē*
a ... car	一辆 ... 车	*yī liàng ... chē*
small	小	*xiǎo*
big	大	*dà*
five-door	五门	*wǔ mén*
for ...	租 ...	*zū ...*
two days	两天	*liǎng tiān*
a week	一个星期	*yī ge xīngqī*
How much is it per day/per week?	一天/一星期多少钱？	*yī tiān/yī xīngqī duō shǎo qián*
Is it unlimited mileage?	不限公里数吗？	*bú xiàn gōnglǐ shù ma*
Is insurance included?	含保险吗？	*hán bǎoxiǎn ma*

Getting **Around**

you may hear ...

租几天?	*zū jǐ tiān*	For how many days?
租多长时间?	*zū duō cháng shíjiān*	For how long?
谁开呢?	*shéi kāi ne*	Who'll be driving?
五十块 ...	*wǔshí kuài ...*	50 kuai ...
一天	*yī tiān*	a day
一星期	*yī xīngqī*	a week
请把 ... 给我看一下。	*qǐng bǎ ... gěi wǒ kàn yīxià*	Your ..., please.
驾照	*jiàzhào*	driving licence
护照	*hùzhào*	passport
需要付押金。	*xūyào fù yājīn*	There's a deposit to pay.

buying petrol

you may say ...

30 litres of/50 yuan of ...	三十升的/五十块的 ...	*sānshi shēng de/wǔshí kuài de ...*
unleaded	无铅汽油	*wúqiān qìyóu*
diesel	柴油	*cháiyóu*
93	九十三号汽油	*jiǔshísān hào qìyóu*
97	九十七号汽油	*jiǔshí qī hào qìyóu*
Which pump is it?	哪个油泵?	*nǎ ge yóubèng*
Have you got any ...	这里 ... 吗?	*zhèlǐ ... ma*
air?	可以打气	*kěyǐ dǎ qì*
water?	可以加水	*kěyǐ jiā shuǐ*
Do you have any ...	有 ... 吗?	*yǒu ... ma*
oil?	车油	*chēyóu*
How much is it?	多少钱?	*duō shǎo qián*

you may hear ...

这里是自助的	*zhèlǐ shì zìzhù de*	It is self-service.
四号油泵	*sì hào yóubèng*	pump number four

on the road

you may say ...

Is this the right way to the Great Wall?	这是去长城的路吗?	*zhè shì qù cháng chéng de lù ma*
How many kilometres to Tianjin?	到天津多少公里?	*dào tiānjīn duō shǎo gōnglǐ*
Is Lanzhou far (from here)?	兰州离这儿远吗?	*lánzhōu lí zhèr yuǎn ma*
How do you get to Changsha?	去长沙怎么走?	*qù chángshā zěnme zǒu*
Can I park here?	这儿可以停车吗?	*zhèr kěyǐ tíngchē ma*
Where is the car park?	停车场在哪儿?	*tíngchē chǎng zài nǎr*

you may hear ...

这条路不去长城。	*zhè tiáo lù bú qù cháng chéng*	This road doesn't lead to the Great Wall.
大约三十公里。	*dàyuē sānshí gōnglǐ*	About 30 kilometres.
不远。	*bù yuǎn*	Not far.
这儿不可以停车。	*zhèr bù kěyǐ tíngchē*	You can't park here.
在加油站旁边。	*zài jiāyóu zhàn pángbiān*	It's next to the petrol station.

road signs

you may see ...

非机动车道	*fēi jīdòng chēdào*	cycle lane
入口	*rùkǒu*	entrance
出口	*chūkǒu*	exit
让	*ràng*	give way
右侧通行	*yòucè tōngxíng*	give way to the right
高速公路	*gāosù gōnglù*	motorway
禁止超车	*jìnzhǐ chāochē*	no overtaking
禁止停车	*jìnzhǐ tíngchē*	no parking
减速慢行	*jiǎnsù màn xíng*	reduce speed

Getting **Around**

taking a taxi

you may say ...

To ... please.	劳驾，去 ... 。	*láo jià, qù ...*
this address	这个地址	*zhè ge dìzhǐ*
the airport	机场	*jīchǎng*
How long will it take?	多长时间能到？	*duō cháng shíjiān néng dào*
How much is it?	多少钱？	*duō shǎo qián*
I need a receipt.	我需要一张收据。	*wǒ xūyào yī zhāng shōujù*

you may hear ...

挺远的。	*tǐng yuǎn de*	It's quite a way.
大约二十分钟。	*dàyuē èrshí fēnzhōng*	About 20 minutes.
很快。	*hěn kuài*	Not long.

check out 2

You take a taxi to the Beijing Hotel.

○ 劳驾，去北京饭店。
  láo jià, qù běijīng fàndiàn

– 好。
  hǎo

○ 多长时间能到？
  duō cháng shíjiān néng dào

– 大约十分钟。
  dàyuē shí fēnzhōng

○ 多少钱？
  duō shǎo qián

– 三十块。
  sānshí kuài

○ 我需要一张收据，谢谢。
  wǒ xūyào yī zhāng shōujù, xièxie

Q How long does it take to get to the Beijing Hotel?
How much does the journey cost?

using the subway

you may say ...

ticket	票	*piào*
monthly pass	月票	*yuè piào*
pay-as-you-go card	充值卡	*chōng zhí kǎ*
One ticket please.	请给我一张票。	*qǐng gěi wǒ yī zhāng piào*
Does this train go to ...?	这趟车去 ... 吗?	*zhè tàng chē qù ... ma*
Which line do I need for ...?	我应该坐几号线去 ...?	*wǒ yīnggāi zuò jǐ hào xiàn qù ...*
Is the next stop ...?	下一站是 ... 吗?	*xià yī zhàn shì ... ma*
Is there access for ...	有 ... 通道吗?	*yǒu ... tōngdào ma*
wheelchairs ?	轮椅	*lúnyǐ*
prams?	婴儿推车	*yīng'ér tuīchē*

you may hear ...

你要在 ... 换车。	*nǐ yào zài ... huàn chē*	You must change at ...
首都体育馆	*shǒudū tǐyùguǎn*	Capital Stadium.
坐 ... 线。	*zuò ... xiàn*	Take line ...
一号	*yī hào*	number one.
在 ... 下车。	*zài ... xià chē*	Get off at ...
王府井	*wángfǔjǐng*	Wangfujing.

getting information

you may say ...

| Are there any trains to ...? | 有去 ... 的火车吗? | *yǒu qù ... de huǒchē ma* |
| the Great Wall | 长城 | *cháng chéng* |

Getting **Around**

Is there ...	有 ... 吗?	*yǒu ... ma*
a shuttle service to the airport?	去机场的班车	*qù jīchǎng de bānchē*
a Maglev to the town centre?	去市中心的磁悬浮	*qù shì zhōngxīn de cíxuánfú*
What time does the flight ...	这趟航班几点 ...	*zhè tàng hángbān jǐ diǎn ...*
take off?	起飞	*qǐ fēi*
land?	着陆	*zhuólù*
What time does it ...	几点 ...	*jǐ diǎn ...*
leave?	发车?	*fāchē*
arrive?	到站?	*dàozhàn*
What time does the next ... leave?	下一趟 ... 几点开?	*xià yī tàng ... jǐ diǎn kāi*
train	火车	*huǒchē*
What time does the last ... leave?	最后一趟 ... 几点开?	*zuìhòu yī tàng ... jǐ diǎn kāi*
bus	公交车; 公共汽车	*gōngjiāochē; gōnggòng qìchē*
boat	船	*chuán*
What number is it?	多少路; 哪一班?	*duōshǎo lù; nǎ yī bān*
Have you got a timetable?	有时刻表吗?	*yǒu shíkèbiǎo ma*
Can I buy a ticket on the bus/tram?	可以在车上买票吗?	*kěyǐ zài chē shàng mǎi piào ma*
Which platform?	哪个站台?	*nǎ ge zhàntái*
Is there a lift?	有电梯吗?	*yǒu diàntī ma*
How long does ... take?	... 要多长时间?	*... yào duō cháng shíjiān*
the flight	坐飞机	*zuò fēijī*
the crossing	坐摆渡	*zuò bǎidù*
the journey	旅途	*lǚtú*
Does it stop at ...?	在 ... 停吗?	*zài ... tíng ma*
Where should I get off?	我应该在哪儿下车?	*wǒ yīnggāi zài nǎr xià chē*
Is food provided?	提供吃的东西吗?	*tígòng chī de dōngxi ma*
Is there a toilet?	有卫生间吗?	*yǒu wèishēngjiān ma*
Where is the left-luggage office?	行李寄存处在哪儿?	*xíngli jìcúnchù zài nǎr*

晚上八点发车。	*wǎnshang bā diǎn fāchē*	It leaves at 8 o'clock in the evening.
在 ... 不停。	*zài ... bù tíng*	It does not stop at ...
我指给你看。	*wǒ zhǐ gěi nǐ kàn*	I'll show you.
你得给我零钱。	*nǐ děi gěi wǒ língqián*	You have to give the exact money.

buying a train ticket

you may say ...

Where's the ticket office, please?	请问，售票处在哪儿？	*qǐng wèn, shòupiào chù zài nǎr*
I'd like a ...	要一张 ...	*yào yī zhāng ...*
return ticket.	往返票。	*wǎngfǎn piào*
single ticket.	单程票。	*dānchéng piào*
for two adults and one child	两张大人，一张小孩儿	*liǎng zhāng dàrén, yī zhāng xiǎoháir*
soft sleeper	软卧	*ruǎn wò*
hard sleeper	硬卧	*yìng wò*
hard seat	硬座	*yìng zuò*
Do you have tickets for tomorrow?	有明天的票吗？	*yǒu míngtiān de piào ma*
I'd like to reserve ...	我想订 ...	*wǒ xiǎng dìng ...*
a seat	一个座位	*yī ge zuòwèi*
a soft sleeper ticket	一张软卧	*yī zhāng ruǎn wò*
Is there a discount for ...	... 优惠吗？	*... yōuhuì ma*
children?	小孩儿	*xiǎoháir*
students?	学生	*xuéshēng*
senior citizens?	老人	*lǎo rén*

Getting **Around**

you may hear …

软卧卖完了。	*ruǎn wò mài wán le*	Soft sleepers are sold out.
硬卧可以吗?	*yìng wò kěyǐ ma*	Will hard sleepers do?
对不起,今天的票卖完了。	*duìbuqǐ, jīntiān de piào mài wán le*	Sorry, today's tickets are sold out.
订票费三十块钱。	*dìngpiào fèi sānshí kuài qián*	There's a 30-yuan booking fee.

check out 3

You're at the station and want to find out about trains to Beijing.

○ 请问,去北京的火车在哪个站台?
 qǐng wèn, qù běijīng de huǒchē zài nǎ ge zhàntái

– 第一站台。
 dì yī zhàntái

○ 几点发车?
 jǐ diǎn fāchē

– 晚上七点。
 wǎnshang qī diǎn

Q Which of the following statements are true?
 a) The train is at platform 7.
 b) The train is at platform 1.
 c) The train leaves at 7pm.

sound check

The sound _x_ is a bit like 'sh' in 'sheep'. To make the correct sound, put the tip of the tongue behind the lower front teeth and try to whistle.

小孩	_xiǎohái_	child/children
学生	_xuéshēng_	student

Practise _x_ with these words:

西	_xī_	west	谢谢	_xièxie_	thank you
小	_xiǎo_	small	下车	_xià chē_	to get off

tone change

When 不 _bù_ 'not' is followed by another fourth tone, it changes to the second tone:

不是	_bú shì_	no

Practise the change of tone from the fourth to the second:

不去	_bú qù_	do not go
不大	_bú dà_	not big

try it out

matching

match the following signs with their English translation:

1	厕所 _cèsuǒ_	**a**	bus station
2	飞机场 _fēijī chǎng_	**b**	airport
3	火车站 _huǒchē zhàn_	**c**	railway station
4	地铁 _dìtiě_	**d**	subway
5	公交车站 _gōngjiāochē zhàn_	**e**	toilet

Getting **Around**

know-how

How might you:

1   speak to a passer-by politely.
2   find out how to get to the railway station.
3   find out if there's a cashpoint close by.
4   ask if you are on the right road to the Great Wall.

a   这附近有提款机吗?
zhè fùjìn yǒu tíkuǎn jī ma

b   对不起; 劳驾; 请问
duìbuqǐ; láo jià; qǐng wèn

c   去火车站怎么走?
qù huǒchē zhàn zěnme zǒu

d   这是去长城的路吗?
zhè shì qù cháng chéng de lù ma

as if you were there

You want to buy a train ticket to the Great Wall. Follow the prompts to play your part.

你好 !
nǐ hǎo

(Say hello and ask for a return ticket to the Great Wall)
对不起，今天的票卖完了。
duìbuqǐ, jīntiān de piào mài wán le

(Ask if they have any tickets for tomorrow)
有。你要几张?
yǒu. nǐ yào jǐ zhāng

(Say you'd like one ticket, and ask if there's a discount for students)
不优惠。
bù yōuhuì

linkup

请问，卫生间在哪儿?	*qǐng wèn, wèishēngjiān zài nǎr*	**Where is** the toilet, please?
附近有加油站吗?	*fùjìn yǒu jiāyóu zhàn ma*	**Is there** a petrol station **near here**?
去 … 怎么走?	*qù … zěnme zǒu*	**How do I get to** …?
几点发车?	*jǐ diǎn fāchē*	**What time** does it leave?
劳驾，去北京饭店。	*láo jià, qù běijīng fàndiàn*	Beijing Hotel, **please**.
我想租一辆车。	*wǒ xiǎng zū yī liàng chē*	**I'd like** to hire a car.

asking questions

Remember to add 吗 *ma* to the end of a sentence to turn it into a yes/no question:

	附近	有	加油站	吗?
	fùjìn	*yǒu*	*jiāyóu zhàn*	*ma*
Lit.	near	have	petrol station	[*ma*]

(Is there a petrol station near here?)

To ask a specific question using a question word, such as 'where', 'when' etc, the word order is the same as a statement. The question word doesn't come first as in English:

	卫生间	在	哪儿?
	wèishēngjiān	*zài*	*nǎr*
Lit.	toilet	is	where

(Where's the toilet?)

For more on forming questions, see the Language Builder, p134. ⤑

Getting **Around**

polite phrases

To ask questions politely, add 请问 *qǐng wèn* at the very beginning of a question:

	请问,	卫生间	在	哪儿?
	qǐng wèn,	*wèishēngjiān*	*zài*	*nǎr*
Lit.	please ask,	toilet	is	where ?

(Where's the toilet, please?)

To make a polite request, start with 劳驾 *láo jià*:

劳驾，三张去青岛的硬卧。
láo jià, sān zhāng qù qīngdǎo de yìng wò
Three hard sleepers to Qingdao, please.

giving directions

When giving directions, Chinese people often use points of the compass: east, south, west and north.

前面红绿灯，往北拐。
*qiǎn miàn hónglǜ dēng, wǎng **běi** guǎi*
Turn north at the traffic lights.

Somewhere **to Stay**

In major cities like Beijing and Shanghai, there are many 5-star (and even 6-star) international chain hotels. Most travel agents dealing with China can book hotels for you, or you can book online. Like in America, the Chinese call the ground floor the first floor, so the UK first floor is the second floor, etc.

hotels and inns

There are several words for hotel, although they are often interchangeable. Hotels must be licensed to accommodate foreigners.

Luxury hotels are called 饭店 (*fàndiàn*), 酒店 (*jiǔdiàn*) or 大酒店 (*dà jiǔdiàn*).

Most luxury hotels accept credit cards. Mid-range and small hotels only accept cash. Rooms are charged per night rather than per person. The quoted room price in 4 or 5-star hotels includes breakfast.

Mid to bottom-range hotels are called 旅店 (*lǚdiàn*), or 旅馆 (*lǚguǎn*). They are used mainly by Chinese people, and sometimes refuse to take foreigners due to government regulations. Here you may have to use shared bathrooms.

Some universities have their own guesthouse 招待所/宾馆 (*zhāodàisuǒ/bīn'guǎn*) for foreign visitors. Be aware that they may be located in the suburbs, some distance from the city centre.

Tap water in most hotels is not drinkable unless stated. Only 5-star hotels provde foreign TV channels. All 4-star hotels and above have internet connection in the room.

Price is not a strictly accurate indication of quality and service. On the whole, the more modern the hotel the higher the standard of service and facilities. In off-season (October – June) price lists are more of a guide, so you can be prepared to bargain anywhere up to 30% off your bill.

service apartments

Service apartments are known as 酒店式公寓 (*jiǔdiànshì gōngyù*) and they are becoming very popular. They are like hotels, but you can ask for an apartment, and they are suitable for families with young children. There are few B&Bs and self-catering flats. If you need accommodation for a longer period, you can rent a room or a flat through an agent.

camping

Camping is a fun, if adventurous, alternative, though due to the size of even the rural populations, privacy can sometimes be an issue. Camping is best in the West of the country. Tibet, Qinghai, and Gansu, have many sites within walking range of small communities.

monasteries

Many monastereries have 'Pilgrims' Inns', offering basic yet affordable accommodation in the countryside.

children

Although children are made very welcome, most hotels do not provide cots.

places to stay

family-style inn	家庭旅馆	*jiātíng lǚguǎn*
guest house	旅馆; 宾馆; 招待所	*lǚguǎn; bīn'guǎn; zhāodàisuǒ*
holiday resort	度假村	*dùjià cūn*
hotel	饭店; 酒店; 大酒店	*fàndiàn; jiǔdiàn; dà jiǔdiàn*
rented room	出租房	*chūzū fáng*
self-catering flat/cottage	自助式公寓/村舍	*zizhùshì gōngyù/cūnshè*
service apartment	酒店式公寓	*jiǔdiànshì gōngyù*
villa	别墅	*biéshù*
youth hostel	青年旅社	*qīngnián lǚshè*

finding a place

you may say ...

Is there ... near here?	附近有... 吗?	*fùjìn yǒu ... ma*
a hotel	酒店	*jiǔdiàn*
youth hostel	青年旅社	*qīngnián lǚshè*
Do you have a room available?	有空房间吗?	*yǒu kòng fángjiān ma*
I'd like a room for ...	我想要一个能住 ... 的房间。	*wǒ xiǎng yào yī ge néng zhù ... de fángjiān*
tonight.	今天一个晚上	*jīntiān yī ge wǎnshang*
three nights.	三个晚上	*sān ge wǎnshang*
a week.	一个星期	*yī ge xīngqī*
a weekend.	一个周末	*yī ge zhōumò*
four people.	四个人	*sì ge rén*
two adults and two children.	两个大人，两个小孩儿	*liǎng ge dàrén, liǎng ge xiǎoháir*
a ... room	一个...	*yī ge ...*
single	单人间	*dānrén jiān*
double	双人间	*shuāngrén jiān*
standard	标准间	*biāozhǔn jiān*
one double bed	一个双人床	*yī ge shuāngrén chuáng*
two single beds	两个单人床	*liǎng ge dānrén chuáng*
May I see the room?	可以看一下房间吗?	*kěyǐ kàn yíxià fángjiān ma*

Somewhere **to Stay**

How much is it per night?	一个晚上多少钱?	*yī gè wǎnshang duō shǎo qián*
Do you have anything cheaper?	有没有便宜一些的?	*yǒu méiyǒu piányi yīxiē de*
Is there a single supplement?	单人间要额外收费吗?	*dānrén jiān yào éwài shōufèi ma*
Can I book online?	可以网上预定吗?	*kěyǐ wǎng shàng yùdìng ma*
I'll think about it.	我考虑一下。	*wǒ kǎolǜ yīxià*
Okay, I'll take it.	好，我要了。	*hǎo, wǒ yào le*

you may hear ...

您想要什么样的房间?	*nín xiǎng yào shénmeyàng de fángjiān*	What sort of room do you want?
住几个晚上?	*zhù jǐ ge waǎnshang*	For how many nights?
几位?	*jǐ wèi*	For how many people?
您要单人间还是双人间?	*nín yào dānrén jiān háishi shuāngrén jiān*	Do you want a single room or a double room?
对不起，客房已满。	*duìbuqǐ, kèfáng yǐ mǎn*	Sorry, we're full.
包午餐或晚餐/半膳	*bāo wǔcān huò wǎncān; bàn shàn*	half board
包早、午、晚三餐/全膳	*bāo zǎo,wǔ,wǎn sān cān; quán shàn*	full board
每一间房	*měi yī jiān fáng*	per room

check out 1

You want to find out if a hotel has a room available.

○ 请问，有双人间吗？
  qǐng wèn, yǒu shuāngrén jiān ma

– 有。
  yǒu

○ 一个晚上多少钱？
  yī ge wǎnshang duō shǎo qián

– 两百四十块。
  liǎng bǎi sìshí kuài

○ 包早餐吗？
  bāo zǎocān ma

– 对不起，不包早餐。
  duìbuqǐ, bù bāo zǎocān

Q What kind of room are you looking for?
How much does it cost per night?

facilities

you may say ...

I'd like a room with a ...	我想要一个带 ... 的房间。	*wǒ xiǎng yào yī ge dài ... de fángjiān*
bathroom.	卫生间	*wèishēngjiān*
shower.	淋浴	*línyù*
Could you add an extra bed?	能不能加一张床？	*néng bu néng jiā yī zhāng chuáng*
Is the bathroom wheelchair-friendly?	有坐轮椅的人用的卫生间吗？	*yǒu zuò lúnyǐ de rén yòng de wèishēngjiān ma*
Is ... included?	包 ...吗？	*bāo ... ma*
breakfast	早餐	*zǎocān*
Onternet access	网费	*wǎng fèi*

Somewhere **to Stay**

Is there ...	有... 吗?	*yǒu ... ma*
a cot?	婴儿床	*ying'ér chuáng*
a lift?	电梯	*diàntī*
an Internet connection/WiFi?	互联网/无线连接	*hùlián wǎng/wúxiàn liánjiē*
room service?	送餐服务	*sòngcān fúwù*

you may hear ...

不包...	*bù bāo ...*	... isn't included.
早餐.	*zǎocān*	Breakfast
...包括在内。	*... bāokuò zàinèi*	... is included.
服务费	*fúwùfèi*	Service charge

checking in
you may say ...

I've got a reservation.	我预订了房间。	*wǒ yùdìng le fángjiān*
My name is ...	我叫 ...	*wǒ jiào ...*
What time ...	...几点?	*... jǐ diǎn*
is breakfast?	早餐是	*zǎocān shì*
Where is the ...	... 在哪儿?	*... zài nǎr*
car park?	停车场	*tíngchē chǎng*
(hotel) restaurant?	餐厅	*cāntīng*
What floor is it on?	在几层?	*zài jǐ céng*
Where can I/we park?	我/我们可以把车停在哪儿?	*wǒ/wǒmen kěyǐ bǎ chē tíng zài nǎr*

you may hear ...

您预订房间了吗?	*nín yùdìng fángjiān le ma*	Have you got a reservation?
请问您的 ...	*qǐng wèn nínde ...*	Your ..., please.
姓名。	*xìngmíng*	name
请出示护照。	*qǐng chūshì húzhào*	passport
您能填一下这张表吗?	*nín néng tián yīxià zhè zhāng biǎo ma*	Could you fill in this form?
您的房间号是二十八号。	*nínde fángjiān hào shì èrshíbā hào*	Your room is number 28.

43

在 … 层	zài … céng	on the … floor
一	yī	ground
二	èr	first
三	sān	second
早餐时间是七点到九点半。	zǎocān shíjiān shì qī diǎn dào jiǔ diǎn bàn	Breakfast is from 7am to 9.30am.
这是钥匙。	zhè shì yàoshi	Here's the key.

you may see …

停车场	tíngchē chǎng	car park
关门	guānmén	closed
请勿打扰	qǐng wù dǎrǎo	do not disturb
男	nán	gentlemen/male
女	nǚ	ladies/female
正在营业	zhèngzài yíngyè	open
餐厅	cāntīng	restaurant

check out 2

You check in to your hotel with a reservation.

○ 您好! 您预订房间了吗?
nín hǎo! nín yùdìng fángjiān le ma

– 预订了。
yùdìng le

○ 请出示您的护照。
qǐng chūshì nínde hùzhào.

– 可以。
kěyǐ

○ 您的房间号是二十六号。 这是钥匙。
nín de fángjiān hào shì èrshíliù hào. zhè shì yàoshi

– 谢谢！
xièxie

Q What do you have to do?
What is your room number?

Somewhere **to Stay**

asking for help

you may say ...

Could I have a wakeup call at ...?	可以在 ... 点提供叫醒服务吗?	*kěyǐ zài... diǎn tígōng jiàoxǐng fúwù ma*
Have you got ...	有...吗?	*yǒu ... ma*
a hairdryer?	吹风机	*chuīfēngjī*
a map of the city?	市区地图	*shìqū dìtú*
a safe?	保险箱	*bǎoxiǎnxiāng*
Could I have ... please?	可以 ... 吗?	*kěyǐ ... ma?*
the key	给我钥匙	*gěi wǒ yàoshi*
another towel	再给我一条毛巾	*zài gěi wǒ yī tiáo máojīn*
another pillow	再给我一个枕头	*zài gěi wǒ yī gè zhěntóu*
Could you ...	你能...吗?	*nǐ néng ... ma*
call a taxi for me?	帮我叫一辆出租车	*bāng wǒ jiào yī liàng chūzūchē*
How do I get an outside number	外线怎么打?	*wàixiàn zěnme dǎ*
How do you work the ...	... 怎么用?	*... zěnme yòng*
fan?	风扇	*fēngshàn*
telephone?	电话	*diànhuà*
There's a problem with ...	... 有毛病了。	*... yǒu máobìng le*
the shower.	淋浴器	*línyùqì*
The ... isn't working.	... 坏了。	*... huài le*
air conditioning	空调	*kōngtiáo*
television	电视	*diànshì*
The room's ...	这个房间 ...。	*zhège fángjiān ...*
too hot.	太热	*tài rè*
very cold.	很冷	*hěn lěng*
There isn't/aren't any ...	没有...。	*méi yǒu ...*
(hot) water.	（热）水	*(rè) shuǐ*
soap.	肥皂	*féizào*
blankets.	毯子	*tǎnzi*
The bathroom is dirty.	浴室很脏。	*yùshì hěn zàng*
It's very noisy.	太吵了。	*tài chǎo le*

拨零。	*bō líng*	Dial zero.
按这个键。	*àn zhè ge jiàn*	You press this button.
我会派人去。	*wǒ huì pài rén qù*	I'll send somebody.
我们会给您送去。	*wǒ men huì gěi nín sòng qù*	We'll get you some.

checking out

you may say ...

I'd like to pay the bill ...	我要结账，...。	*wǒ yào jiézhàng, ...*
by credit card.	用信用卡	*yòng xìnyòng kǎ*
with cash.	用现金	*yòng xiànjīn*
I think there's a mistake.	我觉得有个错。	*wǒ juéde yǒu ge cuò*

you may hear ...

房号是多少?	*fáng hào shì duō shǎo*	What room number?
请给我钥匙。	*qǐng gěi wǒ yàoshi*	The key, please.
您想怎么付款?	*nín xiǎng zěnme fùkuǎn*	How would you like to pay?
请在这儿签名。	*qǐng zài zhèr qiānmíng*	Sign here.
当然可以。	*dāngrán kěyǐ*	Of course you can.

at the service apartment

you may say ...

How much is a... per night?	一套 ... 一个晚上多少钱?	*yī tào ... yī ge wǎnshang duō shǎo qián*
2-bedroom flat	两居室	*liǎng jūshì*
3-bedroom flat	三居室	*sān jūshì*
Where is/are ...	... 在哪儿	*... zài nǎr*
the cutlery	餐具	*cānjù*
the dustbins?	垃圾桶	*lājītǒng*
Can I hire ...	能租给我 ... 吗?	*néng zū gěi wǒ ... ma*
a duvet?	一床被子	*yī chuáng bèizi*
some towels?	几条毛巾	*jī tiáo máojīn*

Somewhere to Stay

you may hear ...

押金每天二十元。	*yājīn měitiān èrshí yuán*	The deposit is 20 yuan per day.
物业管理费每周五十元。	*wùyè guǎnlǐ fèi měi zhōu wǔshí yuán*	The property management fee is 50 yuan per week.

check out 3

You ask about the cost of a two-bedroom service apartment.

○ 有两居室吗？
yǒu liǎng jūshì ma

– 有。您住几个晚上？
yǒu. nín zhù jǐ ge wǎnshang

○ 三个晚上。一天多少钱？
sān ge wǎnshang. yī tiān duō shǎo qián

– 一百五。
yī bǎi wǔ

○ 可以看一下房间吗？
kěyǐ kàn yīxià fángjiān ma

– 可以。
kěyǐ

Q

1 How long would you like to stay?
   a) one day
   b) two days
   c) three days

2 How much does it cost for a two-bedroom flat per day?

sound check

The *ü* sound is a bit like 'o' in 'do'. When *ü* follows *j*, *q*, *x* and *y*, it is written as *u* without the two dots over it, but it is still pronounced as *ü* because the final sound *u* never occurs after *j*, *q*, *x*:

两居室	*liǎng jūshì*	two-bedroom flat
餐具	*cānjù*	cutlery
去	*qù*	to go

Practise saying the *ü* sound

| 旅行 | *lǚxíng* | travel |
| 市区地图 | *shìqū dìtú* | map of the town |

try it out

match it up

Match the English words with their Chinese equivalents.

1 餐厅 *cāntīng*
2 男 *nán*
3 女 *nǚ*
4 请勿打扰 *qǐng wù dǎrǎo*
5 停车场 *tíngchē chǎng*

a car park
b do not disturb
c ladies/female
d gentlemen/male
e restaurant

Somewhere **to Stay**

mind the gap

Complete the conversations using the phrases below.

1 您租几天? *nín zū jǐ tiān*
2 请问，有互联网吗? *qǐng wèn, yǒu hùliánwǎng ma*
3 一天多少钱? *yī tiān duōshǎo qián*
4 可以看一下房间吗? *kěyǐ kàn yīxià fángjiān ma*

a 一百 *yī bǎi*
b 五天 *wǔ tiān*
c 可以 *kěyǐ*
d 对不起，没有 *duìbuqǐ, méi yǒu*

as if you were there

You're looking for a room for two adults. Follow the prompts to take part in the conversation.

(Say excuse me then ask if they have any rooms available)
有，您要单间还是双间?
yǒu, nín yào dān jiān háishì shuāng jiān

(Say a double room with two single beds)
可以。住几个晚上?
kě yǐ, zhù jǐ ge wǎnshang

(Say three nights. Then ask how much it is per night)
三百元，一共九百元。
sān bǎi yuán, yī gòng jiǔ bǎi yuán

(Ask if you can see the room)
当然可以。
dāng rán kěyǐ

49

linkup

有空房间吗?	*yǒu kòng fángjiān ma*	**Do you have** a room available?
有电梯吗?	*yǒu diàntī ma*	**Is there** a lift?
没有热水。	*méi yǒu rè shuǐ*	**There isn't any** hot water.
你能帮我叫一辆出租车吗?	*nǐ néng bāng wǒ jiào yī liàng chūzūchē ma*	**Could you** call a taxi for me?
早餐是几点?	*zǎocān shì jǐ diǎn*	**What time** is breakfast?

adjectives

Some words in Chinese can be used as verbs and adjectives. When they are used as an adjective they come before a noun:

热 水   *rè shuǐ*   hot water

Or they come after a noun and have an additional meaning of 'to be'. Here 热 *rè* means 'be hot':

	这 个	房 间	太	热。
	zhè ge	*fángjiān*	*tài*	*rè*
Lit.	This	room	too	hot.

This room is too hot.

When an adjective is used this way, it is often preceded by phrases such as:

很	*hěn*	very
有点儿	*yǒudiǎnr*	a little
太	*tài*	too

For more on adjectives, see the Language Builder, p131.

Somewhere **to Stay**

negatives

There are two main negation words in Chinese:

不   *bù*
没   *méi*

不 *bù* is used in most instances and is placed directly in front of the verb:

> 不包早餐。
> **bù** *bāo zǎocān*

Lit.   Does not include breakfast.
         Breakfast is not included.

To negate the verb 有 *yǒu* 'to have', 没 *méi* is used before the verb:

> 没有热水。
> **méi** *yǒu rè shuǐ*

Lit.   not have hot water
         There isn't any hot water.

For more on negation, see the Language Builder, p133. ····⟩

verbs

Verbs have only one form, regardless of who or what is doing the action. For example, *qù* means 'to go to':

我去中国。	*wǒ* **qù** *Zhōngguó*	I go to China.
他/她去中国。	*tā* **qù** *Zhōngguó*	He/She goes to China.
我们去中国。	*wǒmen* **qù** *Zhōngguó*	We go to China.

Buying **Things**

opening hours

Most shops and supermarkets are open from 9am to 9pm, seven days a week. Some small shops open until 10pm.

Banks are open from 9am to 5pm. Most banks are open seven days a week. But money changing facilities may not be available at weekends.

department stores

The Chinese phrase for department store is 百货商店 (*bǎihuò shāngdiàn*), the literal translation of which is 'hundreds of goods store'. Most department stores sell all sorts of items, ranging from buttons to televisions. Toiletries can only be bought in department stores, not at the chemist's.

In Beijing, the smart department stores are located in 王府井 (*wángfǔjǐng*), not far from Tian'anmen Sqaure.

In Shanghai, one of the most important commercial and tourist streets is 南京路 (*nánjīng lù*).

There are hundreds of shops, including the city's largest department store.

souvenirs

There are many traditional gifts, ranging from Chinese silk, tea, antiques, paintings and calligraphy, jade and pearls to miniatures of the terracotta army.

The best places to buy souvenirs are art and craft shops, friendship stores or markets. Gift shops that are attached to particular historical sites tend to be rather expensive. The Panjiayuan flea market in Beijing 潘家园 (*pānjiāyuán*) has a good selection of items.

Pearls Shanghai Hongqiao International Pearl City near Shanghai Hongqiao Airport, and Hongqiao Market in Beijing are the best places. Prices are negotiable.

Silk A silk street called 丝绸一条街 (*sīchóu yī tiáo jiē*) in Hangzhou is an excellent place to shop for silk products.

Paintings and calligraphy

The best place to go is 琉璃厂 (*liúlichǎng*) in Beijing. It is a street full of shops that sell paintings, calligraphy and other related items.

markets

There are various kinds of markets – food markets, fish markets, clothes markets, silk markets, pearl markets, etc. Bargaining is acceptable.

The best places to buy food are either from a supermarket or an early morning food market. Get there early as fresh produce is sold out quickly.

quantity

In supermarkets most things are sold in kilos 公斤 (*gōngjīn*). But in markets and small stalls, the old measurements of weight are still in use: 斤 (*jīn*) and 两 (*liǎng*). One jin is half a kilo, and there are 10 liangs in one jin. Even liquids such as soy sauce can be sold by jin.

Light items such as tea and Chinese herbs are sold by the gramme 克 (*kè*).

general phrases

Do you have any ...	有... 吗?	yǒu ... ma
beer?	啤酒	píjiǔ
jasmine tea?	茉莉花茶	mòlìhuā chá
postcards?	明信片	míngxinpiàn
stamps?	邮票	yóupiào
English newspapers?	英文报纸	yīngwén hànzhǐ
How much is ...	... 多少钱?	... duō shǎo qián
that?	那个	nàge
this skirt?	这条裙子	zhè tiáo qúnzi
How much are ...	... 多少钱?	... duō shǎo qián
these chopsticks?	这些筷子	zhèxiē kuàizi
I'd like ... please.	我想买...; 我要 ...	wǒ xiǎng mǎi ...; wǒ yào ...
some sparkling water	一些带气的水	yīxiē dàiqide shuǐ
two postcards	两张明信片	liǎng zhāng míngxin piàn
I'd like another.	我想再要一个。	wǒ xiǎng zài yào yī ge
May I try some?	可以尝尝吗?	kěyǐ chángchang ma
What is it?	这是什么?	zhè shì shénme
this one/that one	这个/那个	zhège/nàge
I'll take it.	我要了。	wǒ yào le
No, nothing else.	不要了。	bú yào le
That's all.	就这些吧。	jiù zhèxiē ba
It's too expensive.	太贵了。	tài guì le
Can I pay ...	能不能 ... 付款?	néng bu néng ... fùkuǎn
by credit card?	用信用卡	yòng xìnyòng kǎ
Could I have a bag, please?	能给我一个袋子吗?	néng gěi wǒ yi ge dàizi ma

需要帮忙吗?	xūyào bāngmáng ma	Can I help you?
抱歉。	bàoqiàn	Sorry.
你要多少?	nǐ yào duō shǎo	How much/many do you want?

Buying **Things**

给你。	*gěi nǐ*	Here you are.
对不起，卖完了。	*duìbuqǐ, mài wán le*	Sorry, it's sold out.
你要吗？	*nǐ yào ma*	Will you take it?
还要别的吗？	*hái yào biéde ma*	Anything else?
够吗？	*gòu ma*	Is that enough?
(共)...元。	*(gong) ... yuán*	That's ... yuan (altogether)
我们只收现金。	*wǒmen zhǐ shōu xiànjīn*	We only accept cash.
这是礼品吗？	*zhè shì lǐpǐn ma*	Is it a present?
需要包装吗？	*xūyào bāozhuāng ma*	Would you like it gift-wrapped?

shops

art and craft shop	工艺品店	*gōngyìpǐn diàn*
bakery	面包店	*miànbāo diàn*
bookshop	书店	*shū diàn*
chemist's	药店	*yào diàn*
Chinese medicine shop	中药店	*zhōng yào diàn*
department store	百货商店	*bǎihuò shāngdiàn*
dry cleaner's	干洗店	*gān xǐ diàn*
early morning food market	早市	*zǎo shì*
food market	农贸市场; 菜市场	*nóngmào shìchǎng; cài shìchǎng*
gold shop	金店	*jīn diàn*
hairdresser's	发廊	*fà láng*
jeweller's	首饰店	*shǒushi diàn*
market	市场	*shìchǎng*
optician's	眼镜店	*yǎnjìng diàn*
photographer's	照相馆	*zhàoxiàng guǎn*
post office	邮局	*yóujú*
shoe shop	鞋店	*xié diàn*
shopping centre	购物中心	*gòuwù zhōngxīn*
silk shop	丝绸店	*sīchóu diàn*
supermarket	超市	*chāoshì*
tailor's	裁缝店	*cáiféng diàn*

quantities

you may say ...

How much is it?	这个多少钱?	*zhège duō shǎo qián*
How much are they ?	这些多少钱?	*zhèxiē duōshǎo qián*
How much is it ...	...多少钱?	*... duō shǎo qián*
per jin?	一斤	*yī jīn*
I'll have ... , please	我要... 。	*wǒ yào ...*
half a jin	半斤	*bàn jīn*
100 grammes	一百克	*yī bǎi kè*
half a jin (250g) ...	半斤...	*bàn jīn ...*
of lychees	荔枝	*lìzhī*
half a kilo of ...	半公斤...	*bàn gōngjīn ...*
a kilo of ...	一公斤...	*yī gōngjīn ...*
apples	苹果	*píngguǒ*
a bit more/less	再多点儿/ 少点儿	*zài duō diǎnr/shǎo diǎnr*
a slice/piece of ...	一片...	*yī piàn*
a bag/packet of ...	一袋...	*yī dài*
a bottle of ...	一瓶...	*yī píng*

check out 1

You're at a tea shop.

○ 有茉莉花茶吗?
  yǒu mòlìhuā chá ma

– 这就是茉莉花茶。
  zhè jiù shì mòlìhuā chá

○ 我要半斤。
  wǒ yào bàn jīn

– 够吗?
  gòu ma

○ 就这些吧。
  jiù zhèxiē ba

Q What kind of tea do you buy?
How much do you buy?

Buying **Things**

fruit & vegetables

apples	苹果	*píngguǒ*
apricots	杏	*xìng*
bananas	香蕉	*xiāngjiāo*
cherries	樱桃	*yīngtao*
dates	枣	*zǎo*
grapes	葡萄	*pútao*
lemon	柠檬	*níngméng*
lettuce	生菜	*shēngcài*
lotus root	莲藕	*lián ǒu*
lychees	荔枝	*lìzhī*
melon	甜瓜	*tiánguā*
orange	橘子	*júzi*
peach	桃子	*táozi*
pear	梨	*lí*
(red/green) pepper	(红/青) 辣椒	*(hóng/qīng) làjiāo*
persimmon	柿子	*shìzi*
pineapple	菠萝	*bōluó*
plum	李子	*lǐzi*
strawberries	草莓	*cǎoméi*
tomato	西红柿; 番茄	*xīhóngshì; fānqié*
watermelon	西瓜	*xīguā*

check out 2

You're at a food market, buying some fruit.

○ 我要一斤苹果，一斤香蕉。
　 wǒ yào yī jīn píngguǒ, yī jīn xiāngjiāo

– 还要别的吗？
　 hái yào biéde ma

○ 不要了。 多少钱？
　 bú yào le. duō shǎo qián

– 一共六块。
　 yī gòng liù kuài

Q What fruit do you want?
How much do you pay?

fish & meat

beef	牛肉	*niúròu*
chicken	鸡肉	*jīròu*
duck	鸭肉	*yāròu*
fish	鱼肉	*yúròu*
meat	肉	*ròu*
prawns/king prawns	虾/大虾	*xiā/dàxiā*
pork	猪肉	*zhūròu*
salmon	三文鱼	*sānwényú*
tuna	吞拿鱼/金枪鱼	*tūnnáyú/jīnqiāngyú*

(see menu reader pp82–89 for more food vocabulary)

groceries

eggs	鸡蛋	*jīdàn*
fruit juice	果汁	*guǒ zhī*
milk	牛奶	*niúnǎi*
mineral water	矿泉水	*kuàngquán shuǐ*
washing powder	洗衣粉	*xǐyī fěn*

Buying **Things**

buying clothes

you may say ...

I'm just looking.	我随便看看。	*wǒ suíbiàn kànkan*
I'd like ...	我想买...。	*wǒ xiǎng mǎi ...*
a shirt.	(一) 件衬衫	*(yī) jiàn chènshān*
a pair of trousers.	(一) 条裤子	*(yī) tiáo kùzi*
a silk dressing gown.	(一) 件真丝睡衣	*(yī) jiàn zhēnsī shuìyī*
in ...		
wool	羊毛的	*yángmáo de*
cotton	棉的	*mián de*
pure silk	真丝的	*zhēn sī de*
leather	皮的	*pí de*
I need the ... size.	我需要 ...号的。	*wǒ xūyào ... hào de*
small	小	*xiǎo*
medium	中	*zhong*
large	大	*dà*
extra large	加大	*jiā dà*
Can I try it/them on?	我可以试试吗?	*wǒ kěyǐ shìshi ma*
It's too ...	太...了。	*tài ... le*
small.	小	*xiǎo*
big.	大	*dà*
Do you have anything ...	有... 吗?	*yǒu ... ma*
smaller?	小一点儿的	*xiǎo yìdiǎnr de*
bigger?	大一点儿的	*dà yìdiǎnr de*
cheaper?	便宜一点儿的	*piányi yìdiǎnr de*
Do you have it in yellow?	有黄色的吗?	*yǒu huángsè de ma?*
I like it.	我喜欢这个。	*wǒ xǐhuān zhège*
I like it but ...	我喜欢，不过 ...	*wǒ xǐhuān, búguò ...*
I don't like it.	我不喜欢这个。	*wǒ bù xǐhuān zhège*
It fits.	很合身。	*hěn héshēn*
It doesn't fit.	不太合身。	*bú tài héshēn*
I'll take it.	我要了。	*wǒ yào le*
I'll think about it.	我再考虑一下。	*wǒ zài kǎolǜ yīxià*

you may hear ...

你要什么？	*nǐ yào shénme*	What would you like to have?
请等一下。	*qǐng děng yīxià*	Please wait a moment.
多大号的（衣服/鞋）？	*duō dà hào de (yīfu/ xié)*	What size? (clothes/shoes)
什么颜色？	*shénme yánsè*	What colour?
你喜欢吗？	*nǐ xǐhuān ma*	Do you like it/them?
你试试吧。	*nǐ shìshi ba*	Try it/them on.
可以	*kěyǐ*	You can/may.

clothes & accessories

(hand) bag	（手提）包	*(shǒutí) bāo*
belt	皮带	*pídài*
blouse	上衣	*shàngyī*
boots	靴子	*xuēzi*
coat	外套	*wàitào*
dress	连衣裙; 套裙	*liányīqún; tàoqún*
gloves	手套	*shǒutào*
hat	帽子	*màozi*
jacket	夹克	*jiákè*
jumper	套头衫	*tàotóushān*
necklace	项链	*xiàngliàn*
purse/wallet	钱包	*qiánbāo*
ring	戒指	*jièzhǐ*
scarf	围巾	*wéijīn*
shirt	衬衣	*chènyī*
skirt	裙子	*qúnzi*
socks	袜子	*wàzi*
swimming costume/ trunks	游泳衣/裤	*yóuyǒng yī/kù*
tie	领带	*lǐngdài*
trousers	裤子	*kùzi*
watch	手表	*shǒubiǎo*
a pair of (shoes)	一双（鞋子）	*yī shuāng (xiézi)*
a pair of (earrings)	一对（耳环）	*yī duì (ěrhuán)*

colours

black	黑色（的）	*hēisè (de)*
blue	蓝色（的）	*lánsè (de)*
brown	棕色（的）	*zōngsè (de)*
green	绿色（的）	*lǜsè (de)*
grey	灰色（的）	*huīsè (de)*
orange	橘色（的）	*júsè (de)*
pink	粉色（的）	*fěnsè (de)*
red	红色（的）	*hóngsè (de)*
white	白色（的）	*báisè (de)*
yellow	黄色（的）	*huángsè (de)*
dark	深色（的）	*shēnsè (de)*
light	浅色（的）	*qiǎnsè (de)*
plain	素色（的）	*sùsè (de)*

check out 3

You want to try on some trousers.

○ 你喜欢吗？
nǐ xǐhuān ma

– 我喜欢，不过太小了
wǒ xǐhuān, búguò tài xiǎo le

○ 这条大，你试试吧。
zhè tiáo dà, nǐ shìshi ba

– 谢谢。
xièxie

Q Do you like the trousers?
What is wrong with the first pair?

at the department store

you may say ...

Where's the ... department?	... 在哪儿?	... zài nǎr
children's	儿童用品	értóng yòngpǐn
women's	女士用品	nǚshì yòngpǐn
men's	男士用品	nánshì yòngpǐn
Which floor are ...	... 在几层?	... zài jǐ céng
toys?	玩具	wánjù
electronic goods?	电器用品	diànqì yòngpǐn
Where can I find ...	在哪儿能找到 ...?	zài nǎr néng zhǎodào ...
leather goods?	皮具	píjù
beauty products?	美容用品	měiróng yòngpǐn
Is there ...	有...吗?	yǒu ... ma
a lift?	电梯	diàntī
Where do I pay?	在哪儿付钱?	zài nǎr fù qián

you may hear ...

在地下	zài dìxià	in the basement
在一层	zài yī céng	on the ground floor
在二/三层	zài èr/sān céng	on the first/second floor
就在那儿	jiù zài nàr	over there

toiletries

condoms	避孕套	bìyùntào
deodorant	腋下喷剂	yèxiàpēnjì
disposable razors	一次性剃须刀	yīcìxìng tìxūdāo
moisturiser	护肤霜	hùfūshuāng
nappies	婴儿尿布	yīng'ér niàobù
sanitary towels	卫生巾	wèishēng jīn
shampoo	洗发液	xǐfàyè
shaving cream	剃须液	tìxūyè
soap	香皂	xiāngzào
tampons	月经棉塞	yuèjīng miánsāi
toothpaste	牙膏	yágāo

Buying **Things**

at the post office
you may say ...

How much is ...?	...多少钱?	... duō shǎo qián
a stamp for the UK	寄到英国的邮票	jì dào yīngguó de yóupiào
a letter	一封信	yī fēngxìn
a postcard	一张明信片	yī zhāng míngxìnpiàn
I'd like to send this to Australia.	我想把这个寄到澳大利亚。	wǒ xiǎng bǎ zhège jì dào àodàlìyà

you may hear ...

六块八。	liù kuài bā	Six yuan and eight jiao.
需要称一下。	xūyào chēng yīxià	It needs weighing.
要纪念邮票吗?	yào jìniàn yóupiào ma	Would you like special stamps?

photography
you may say ...

Can you print from this memory card?	能打印记忆卡吗?	néng dǎyìn jìyì kǎ ma
When will it be ready?	什么时候能好?	shénme shíhòu néng hǎo
Do you sell... disposable cameras?	有... 吗? 一次性相机	yǒu ... ma yīcìxìng xiàngjī

you may hear ...

多大的?	duō dà de	What size?
绒面的还是光面的?	róngmiàn de háishì guāngmiàn de	Matt or gloss?
今天/ 明天	jīntiān/míngtiān	today/tomorrow
... 以后	...yǐ hòu	in ...
一小时	yī xiǎoshí	one hour
三天	sān tiān	three days

sound check

The sound *q* is similar to 'ch' in 'chin':

矿泉水	*kuàngquán shuǐ*	mineral water
裙子	*qúnzi*	skirt
钱包	*qiánbāo*	wallet

Practise the *q* sound in the following words:

套裙	*tàoqún*	dress
多少钱?	*duōshǎo qián*	How much is it?
七十七	*qīshíqī*	seventy-seven

try it out

match it up

Match the questions with the answers.

1 什么时候能好? *shénme shíhòu néng hǎo*
2 多少钱一斤? *duō shǎo qián yī jīn*
3 能不能用信用卡付款? *néng bu néng yòng xìnyòng kǎ fùkuǎn*
4 有没有英文报纸? *yǒu méi yǒu yīngwén bàozhǐ*

a 对不起，卖光了。 *duìbuqǐ, mài guāng le*
b 明天 *míngtiān*
c 不能，我们只收现金。 *bù néng, wǒmen zhǐ shōu xiànjīn*
d 六块八 *liù kuài bā*

order, order

Put the units of weight in order, the lightest first.

1 斤 *jīn*
2 公斤 *gōngjīn*
3 两 *liǎng*
4 克 *kèǐ*

as if you were there

You are browsing at a market and see a jacket you like.

你要什么?
nǐ yào shénme
(Say that you are just looking)
你喜欢这件真丝睡衣吗?
nǐ xǐhuān zhè jiàn zhēnsī shuìyī ma
(Ask if you can try it on)
当然可以。
dāng rán kěyǐ
(Ask if she has it in black)
有,请等一下。
yǒu, qǐng děng yī xià

linkup

有邮票吗?	*yǒu yóupiào ma*	**Do you have** any stamps?
我想买(一)件真丝睡衣。	*wǒ xiǎng mǎi (yī) jiàn zhēnsī shuìyī*	**I'd like** a silk dressing gown.
儿童用品在哪儿?	*értóng yòngpǐn zài nǎr*	**Where's** the children's department?
这双鞋多少钱?	*zhè shuāng xié duō shǎo qián*	**How much is** this pair of shoes?
有大一点儿的吗?	*yǒu dà yīdiǎnr de ma*	Do you have anything **bigger**?
你喜欢吗? 喜欢。	*nǐ xǐhuān ma xǐhuān*	Do you **like** it? Yes, I **like** it.

comparing things

To make comparisons add 一点儿 *yīdiǎnr* after the adjective:

小	*xiǎo*	small
小一点儿	*xiǎo yīdiǎnr*	smaller
大	*dà*	big
大一点儿	*dà yīdiǎnr*	bigger
便宜	*piányi*	cheap
便宜一点儿	*piányi yīdiǎnr*	cheaper

Buying **Things**

singular and plural

Nouns in Chinese have no singular and plural distinctions:

一条裙子 *yī tiáo qúnzi* one skirt
三条裙子 *sān tiáo qúnzi* three skirts

There are no articles ('a', 'an', 'the') in Chinese. *Wǒ qù mǎi dìtú* can mean 'I'm going to buy a map' or 'I'm going to buy the map'. The context and measure words will help to clarify the meaning.

yī one + measure word
zhè/nà (this/that) + measure word

number one

If you want to say 'I'd like to buy one skirt', you can omit the number word for 'one' — *yī* before the measure word, in this example 条 *tiáo*:

我想买 (一)条裙子。 *wǒ xiǎng mǎi (yī) tiáo qúnzi*
I'd like to buy a skirt.

Other numbers can't be omitted:

我想买三条裙子。 *wǒ xiǎng mǎi **sān** tiáo qúnzi*
I'd like to buy three skirts.

Eating **Out**

More and more restaurants offer menus in both English and Chinese, but the majority still only have the menu in Chinese.

Table manners are not an issue. It is accepted etiquette for people to reach across the dining table for food, soy sauce, salt, pepper, etc.

Tipping is not expected, as service is usually included. Culturally it is not acceptable to divide the bill. Most restaurants will provide you with boxes to take leftovers home.

when to eat

Chinese people usually have dinner around 6pm. So by 9pm, most restaurants are empty, and some popular dishes are not available.

If you are invited to eat at a Chinese friend's house for a meal, turn up 10 to 20 minutes earlier than the agreed time.

where to eat

Most small to medium-sized Chinese restaurants only use chopsticks, knives and forks are not available. Some restaurants offer a wide range of dishes, some specialise in a particular style of cuisine, eg Sichuan cuisine. Others specialise in specific dishes: noodles, dumplings, roast duck, barbecued food, etc.

Big cities will also have restaurants offering cuisine from other Asian countries, especially Korean, Japanese and Thai.

In Beijing, Shanghai and Guangzhou, western restaurants are on the increase, look for 西式 餐厅 (*xīshì cāntīng*).

courses

A typical breakfast consists of rice porridge, steamed bread with preserved vegetables or salted eggs. Soya milk and deep-fried bread sticks are also popular.

A typical Chinese meal consists of some cold dishes, and sometimes soup to start with, followed by any hot dishes that have been ordered, together with rice or noodles.

Often the dishes are ordered together, and shared among everyone at the table.

Most Chinese people don't have a dessert after their meal, sometimes sweet snacks such as almond cakes accompany the hot dishes. Some larger restaurants may serve pieces of fruit.

what to try

There are regional differences in Chinese cuisine.

Sichuan food is famous for its use of chilli and pepper
Cantonese food emphasises freshness, and the flavour is mild.

drinks

Most Chinese people have tea with their meals. There are three main types of tea: black tea 红茶 (*hóng chá*), green tea 绿茶 (*lǜ chá*) and jasmine tea 花茶 (*huā chá*).

酒 (*jiǔ*) refers to all alcoholic drinks, including spirits, wine and beer. Sweet wine is more popular than dry wine, and red is more popular than white wine.

dietary requirements

Most restaurants use monosodium glutamate 味精 (*wèijīng*) in their cooking. So if you are allergic to it, tell them not to use it. Most tap water is not drinkable.

vegetarians

There aren't many vegetarian restaurants, but most places will have a wide range of vegetable and soy-based dishes.

children

Children's menus don't exist in China. Children eat the same as adults.

finding somewhere to eat

you may say ...

Is there a good restaurant nearby?	附近有好一点儿的餐馆吗？	*fùjìn yǒu hǎo yī diǎnr de cānguǎn ma*
Can you recommend a ... restaurant?	你能推荐一家 ...吗？	*nǐ néng tuījiàn yī jiā ... ma*
Sichuan	四川饭馆	*sìchuān fànguǎn*
Korean	韩国餐	*hánguó cān*
buffet style	自助餐	*zizhù cān*
noodle bar	面馆	*miàn guǎn*
fast food	快餐	*kuài cān*
grill/barbecue	烧烤	*shāokǎo*
I'd like to book a table for ...	我想订个桌，... 。	*wǒ xiǎng dìng ge zhuō ...*
tomorrow night.	明天晚上的	*míngtiān wǎnshang de*
this evening at 8.30pm.	今天晚上八点半的	*jīntiān wǎnshang bā diǎn bàn de*
four people.	四个人的	*sì ge rén de*

arriving

you may say ...

Do you have ...	有...吗？	*yǒu ... ma*
a table for two?	两人桌	*liǎng rén zhuō*
a high chair?	儿童高椅子	*értóng gāo yǐzi*
I have a reservation for four people.	我订了个桌，四个人的。	*wǒ dìng le ge zhuō, sì ge rén de*
It's in the name of ...	订餐人是...。	*dìng cān rén shì ...*
How long do we have to wait?	需要等多久？	*xūyào děng duō jiǔ*

you may hear ...

欢迎光临!	*huānyíng guānglín*	Welcome!
抱歉，今天晚上没有位置了。	*bàoqiàn, jīntiān wǎnshang méi yǒu wèizhì le*	Sorry, we're full tonight.
半小时后再来吧。	*bàn xiǎoshí hòu zài lái ba*	Come back in about half an hour.
你得等一会儿。	*nǐ děi děng yīhuìr*	You'll have to wait.

Eating **Out**

asking about the menu
you may say ...

The menu, please.	请给我菜单看一下。	*qǐng gěi wǒ càidān kàn yī xià*

Do you have ...
  the menu in English?
	有... 吗?
	  英文菜单
		yǒu ... ma
		  yīnwén càidān

What's ...
  the local speciality?
  the speciality of your restaurant?
	... 是 什么?
	  当地特菜
	  你们饭店的特菜
		... shì shénme
		  jdāngdì tècài
		  nǐmen fàndiàn de tècài

What do you recommend?	你推荐什么菜?	*nǐ tuījiàn shénme cài*

Have you got any ...
  dumplings?
  vegetarian dishes?
	有... 吗?
	  饺子
	  素食
		yǒu ... ma
		  jiǎozi
		  sù shí

What's the local speciality?	有什么小吃?	*yǒu shénme xiǎochī*
What's this?	这是什么?	*zhè shì shénme*
How is it cooked?	怎么做的?	*zěnme zuò de*

Is it ...
  strong?
  spicy?
	这个菜...吗?
	  味道很重
	  很辣
		zhè ge cài ... ma
		  wèidào hěn zhòng
		  hěn là

Does it contain ...
  meat?
  nuts?
  wheat?
	里面有没有 ...?
	  肉
	  果仁
	  大麦
		lǐmiàn yǒu méi yǒu ...
		  ròu
		  guǒrén
		  dàmài

I'm allergic to ...
  MSG.
  seafood.
	我对... 过敏。
	  味精
	  海鲜
		wǒ duì ... guòmǐn
		  wèijīng
		  hǎixiān

Please don't put MSG in my dish.	请不要放味精。	*qǐng bú yào fàng wèijīng*
I'm vegetarian.	我是个素食者。	*wǒ shì ge sùshízhě*
What sort of snacks have you got?	你们有什么小吃?	*nǐmén yǒu shénme xiǎochī*

你想要点儿什么?	nǐ xiǎng yào diǎnr shénme	What would you like?
今天有 ...	jīntiān yǒu ...	Today, we have ...
里面没有肉。	lǐmiàn méi yǒu ròu	There isn't any meat in it.

这是...。
  一种蘑菇
	zhè shì ...
	  yī zhǒng mógū
		It's ...
		  a type of mushroom.

你们想要点儿小吃吗?	nǐ mén xiǎng yào diǎnr xiǎochī ma	Would you like to have any snacks?

有 ... 。
  宫廷点心
  豌豆糕
	yǒu ...
	  gōng tíng diǎnxīn
	  wāntóu gāo
		We have ...
		  Palace style cakes.
		  pea cakes.

ordering

I'll have ...
  that.
  the 200-yuan set menu.
	我要... 。
	  那个
	  两百元的套餐
		wǒ yào ...
		  nàge
		  liǎng bǎi yuán de tào cān

We won't have cold dishes.	我们不要凉菜。	wǒmen bú yào liáng cài
We'll just have some hot dishes.	我们只想要几个热菜。	wǒmen zhǐ xiǎng yào jǐ ge rè cài

without ...
  mushrooms
  bean sprouts
	没有...
	  蘑菇
	  豆芽
		méi yǒu ...
		  mógū
		  dòu yá

What's in this?	这里面是什么?	zhè lǐmiàn shi shénme

Eating **Out**

How many dumplings are there in each portion?	一份饺子有几个？	*yī fèn jiǎozi yǒu jǐ ge*
A portion of ... , please.	请来一份 ...	*qǐng lái yī fèn...*
Yes, please.	要，谢谢。	*yào, xièxie*
No, thank you.	不要，谢谢。	*bú yào, xièxie*

you may hear...

现在点菜吗？	*xiànzài diǎn cài ma*	Are you ready to order?
喝点儿什么？	*hē diǎnr shénme*	Anything to drink?
我会告诉厨房的。	*wǒ huì gàosu chúfáng de*	I'll tell the kitchen.
饺子和火锅是这儿的特菜。	*jiǎozi hé huǒguō shì zhèr de tècài*	Dumplings and hot pot are the speciality here.
一份十个。	*yī fèn shí ge*	Ten in each portion.
慢用！	*màn yòng*	Enjoy your meal!

check out 1

You're ordering a meal.

○ 现在点菜吗？
xiànzài diǎn cài ma

– 点。你们饭店的特菜是什么？
diǎn. nǐmen fàndiàn de tècài shì shénme

○ 饺子和火锅是这儿的特菜。
jiǎozi hé huǒguō shì zhèr de tècài

– 我们要火锅。请不要放味精。
wǒmen yào huǒguō. qǐng bú yào fàng wèijīng

Q What is the speciality of this restaurant?
What's your special requirement for your dish?

drinks

you may say ...

The drinks list, please.	请给我酒水单。	*qǐng gěi wǒ jiǔ shuǐ dān*
What kind of tea do you have?	你们有什么茶?	*(nǐmen) yǒu chá ma*
I'd like to have ... jasmine tea.	我想喝... 茉莉花茶。	*wǒ xiǎng hē ... mòlihuā chá*
I'll have ... black tea. a beer.	我要... 红茶。 一个啤酒。	*wǒ yào ... hóng chá yī ge píjiǔ*
Do you have ... coffee? Chinese spirit (like vodka) wine mineral water	(你们)有...吗? 咖啡 白酒 葡萄酒 矿泉水	*(nǐmen) yǒu ... ma kāfēi bái jiǔ pútaojiǔ kuàngquán shuǐ*
a glass	一杯	*yī bēi*
bottle	一瓶	*yī píng*
half a bottle	半瓶	*bàn píng*

you may hear ...

喝点儿什么茶?	*hē diǎnr shénme chá*	What kind of tea would you like?
我们没有进口啤酒。	*wǒmen méi yǒu jìnkǒu píjiǔ*	We don't have any imported beer.
有当地啤酒。	*yǒu dāngdì píjiǔ*	We have local beer.
对不起，没有...	*duìbuqǐ, méi yǒu ...*	Sorry, we don't have ...

(For more drinks, see the menu reader pp88–89.)

Eating **Out**

during the meal

you may say ...

Excuse me!	对不起！	*duìbuqǐ*
Excuse me, is our food coming soon?	劳驾，我们的菜快来了吗？	*láo jià, wǒmen de cài kuài lái le ma*
I've been waiting for half an hour!	我已经等了半个钟头了!	*wǒ yǐjīng děng le bàn ge zhōngtóu le*
I didn't order ...	我没点...	*wǒ méi diǎn ...*
this.	这个。	*zhège*
rice.	米饭。	*mǐfàn*
Another ...	再来...	*zài lái ...*
beer.	一瓶啤酒	*yī píng píjiǔ*
More ..., please.	(请)再来点儿...	*qǐng zài lái diǎnr ...*
rice	米饭。	*mǐfàn*
water	水。	*shuǐ*
It's delicious/very good.	真香/真好吃。	*zhēn xiāng/zhēn hǎochī*
It's ...	这个有点儿...	*zhège yǒu diǎnr...*
cold.	凉。	*liáng*
tough.	硬。	*yìng*
The dumplings are for me.	饺子是我点的。	*jiǎozi shì wǒ diǎn de*
Where are the toilets?	卫生间在哪儿?	*wèishēngjiān zài nǎr*

you may hear ...

你想... 吗?	*nǐ xiǎng ... ma*	Would you like me to ...
现在就上热菜	*xiànzài jiù shàng rè cài*	serve the hot dishes now?
还要点儿什么?	*hái yào diǎnr shénme*	Would you like anything else?
请稍等。	*qǐng shāo děng*	Please wait a moment.
饭菜味道怎么样?	*fàn cài wèidào zěnmeyàng*	Is everything all right?
吃完了吗?	*chī wán le ma*	Have you finished?

check out 2

Your meal isn't going smoothly.

○ 饭菜味道怎么样？
fàn cài wèidào zěnmeyàng

– 真好吃，谢谢！
zhēn hǎochī, xièxie

○ 还要点儿什么？
hái yào diǎnr shénme

– 你们有咖啡吗？
nǐmen yǒu kāfēi ma

○ 对不起，没有咖啡。
duìbuqǐ, méi yǒu kāfēi

Q Are you happy with the meal?
What else do you want?

on your table

ashtray	烟灰缸	*yānhuīgāng*
chopsticks	筷子	*kuàizi*
cup	茶杯	*chábēi*
fork	叉子	*chāzi*
glass	玻璃杯	*bōlibēi*
(fish) knife	（鱼）刀	*(yú) dāo*
napkin	餐巾纸	*cānjīnzhǐ*
plate	盘子	*pánzi*
soup spoon	汤勺	*tāng sháo*
serving spoon	公勺	*gōng sháo*
tablecloth	桌布	*zhuōbù*
soy sauce	酱油	*jiàngyóu*
vinegar	醋	*cù*

paying the bill

you may say ...

The bill, please.	劳驾，请结账。	*láo jià, qǐng jiézhàng*
Can we have the bill please?	可以结账吗?	*kěyǐ jiézhàng ma*
Do you take credit cards?	可以用信用卡吗?	*kěyǐ yòng xìnyòngkǎ ma*
Is service included?	服务费包括在内吗?	*fúwùfèi bāokuò zài nèi ma*
There's a mistake, I think.	我觉得这儿有个错。	*wǒ juéde zhèr yǒu ge cuò*

We didn't have ...
  any beer.
  this cold dish.
	我们没有要... 。
	  啤酒
	  这种凉菜
		wǒmen méiyǒu yào ...
		  píjiǔ
		  zhè zhǒng liáng cài

you may hear ...

好的，就来。	*hǎode, jiù lái*	Okay, I'll be with you soon.
这是你的账单。	*zhè shi nǐde zhàngdān*	Here's your bill.
服务费包括在内。	*fúwùfèi bāokuò zài nèi*	Service is included.
对不起，我们这儿不收信用卡。	*duìbuqǐ, wǒmen zhèr bù shōu xìnyòng kǎ*	Sorry, we do not accept credit cards.
我们只收现金。	*wǒmen zhǐ shōu xiànjīn*	We only accept cash.

sound check

The sound *er* is pronounced a bit like 'ur' in 'fur', but with the tongue rolled back producing the 'l' sound in 'all'. It is a distinctive feature of Mandarin Chinese, and the *er* is often written in pinyin without the *e*:

| 一会儿 | *yīhuì'er* → *yīhuìr* | a while |
| 这儿 | *zhè'er* → *zhèr* | here |

Practise with the following *er* sounds at the end of the syllable:

哪儿	*nǎ'er* → *nǎr*	where
那儿	*nà'er* → *nàr*	there
有点儿	*yǒu diǎn'er* → *yǒu diǎnr*	to have a little/a little
一点儿	*yìdiǎn'er* → *yìdiǎnr*	a little

try it out

match it up

Match the questions with the right answers.

1 还要点儿什么?   *hái yào diǎnr shénme*
   a 对不起。   *duìbuqǐ*
   b 再要一份饺子。   *zài yào yī fèn jiǎozi*

2 现在就上热菜吗?   *xiànzài jiù shàng rè cài ma*
   a 好的,谢谢。   *hǎode, xièxie*
   b 不要放味精。   *bú yào fàng wèijīng*

3 喝点儿什么?   *hē diǎnr shénme*
   a 一瓶啤酒,一瓶矿泉水。   *yī píng píjiǔ, yī píng kuàngquán shuǐ*
   b 一个冰淇淋。   *yī ge bīngqílín*

Eating **Out**

menu mix-up
Put each of the dishes below in the right group: 1 breakfast, 2 cold dishes and 3 hot dishes, (use the Menu Reader pp82–89).

1	早餐	*zǎocān*
2	凉菜	*liángcài*
3	热菜	*rècài*

a	糖醋排骨	*táng cù páigǔ*
b	卤水拼盘	*lǔ shuǐ pīn pán*
c	蛋炒饭	*dàn chǎo fàn*
d	香干马兰头	*xiāng gān mǎlántóu*
e	饺子	*jiǎozi*
f	咖啡	*kāfēi*
g	煎鸡蛋	*jiān jīdàn*
h	豆芽炒面	*dòu yá chǎo miàn*
i	油焖大虾	*yóumèn dàxiā*
j	烤面包	*kǎo miànbāo*

as if you were there
You're in a restaurant and ask the waiter for the bill. Follow the prompts below.

(Say excuse me, and ask for the bill)
好的，就来。这是你的账单。
hǎode, jiù lái. zhè shì nǐde zhàngdān

(Say that you think there's a mistake, you didn't have any beer)
对不起。
duìbuqǐ.

(Say that's alright, and ask if you can pay by credit card)
对不起，我们只收现金。
duìbuqǐ, wǒmen zhǐ shōu xiànjīn

linkup

我想订个桌。	*wǒ xiǎng dìng ge zhuō*	**I'd like** to book a table.
有素食吗?	*yǒu sù shí ma*	**Do you have** any vegetarian dishes?
这是什么?	*zhè shì shénme*	**What's** this?
我要一个豆腐汤。	*wǒ yào yī ge dòufu tāng*	**I'll have** the tofu soup.
我没点米饭。	*wǒ méi diǎn mǐfàn*	**I did not** order rice.
请再加点儿水。	*qǐng zài jiā diǎnr shuǐ*	**More** water, please.
我对味精过敏。	*wǒ duì wèijīn guòmǐn*	**I'm allergic to** MSG.

'Do you have ...?'

When asking 'Do you have ...?' or 'Have you got ...?' both are translated as 有... 吗? *yǒu ... ma*. The word for 'you' 你 *nǐ* is often omitted:

有素食吗?   *yǒu sùshí ma*   Do you have any vegetarian dishes?

In formal situations the plural pronoun for 'you' 你们 *nǐmen* can be used, rather than the singular form 你 *nǐ*:

你们有咖啡吗?   *nǐmen yǒu kāfēi ma*   Have you got any coffee?

Read more about pronouns in the Language Builder, p132.

negation

We have mentioned ealier that the negation word 没 *méi* meaning 'not' is used to negate the verb 'to have' 有 *yǒu*. It is also used to negate things that did not happen in the past or have not happened yet:

我们没点米饭。	*wǒmen **méi** diǎn mǐfàn*	We did not order rice.

please and thank you

The Chinese equivalent of 'Yes, please' in response to an offer is to repeat the verb used in the original offer and add 'thank you' 谢谢 *xièxie*. The word for 'please' 请 *qǐng* is never used for this purpose:

现在点菜吗？	*xiànzài **diǎn** cài ma*	Are you ready to order?
点，谢谢。	*diǎn, xièxie*	Yes, please.

To say 'No, thank you', add 不 *bù* in front of the main verb used in the question and then say 'thank you':

现在点菜吗？	*xiànzài **diǎn** cài ma*	Are you ready to order?
不点，谢谢	*bù diǎn, xièxie*	No, thank you.

Menu **Reader**

courses

凉菜/头盘	liáng cài/tóu pán	cold dishes/starters
热菜/正餐	rè cài/zhèng cān	hot dishes/main course
汤	tāng	soup
早餐	zǎocān	breakfast
午餐	wǔcān	lunch
晚餐	wǎncān	dinner
小吃	xiǎochī	snacks
早茶	zǎochá	dim sum
自助餐	zìzhùcān	buffet

main cooking styles

炖	dùn	braised in low heat
红烧	hóng shāo	braised in soy sauce
焖	mèn	braised with lid on
广东菜	guǎngdōng cài	Canton cuisine
炸	zhá	deep fried
煎	jiān	fried in shallow oil
福建菜	fújiàn cài	Fujian cuisine
火锅	huǒ guō	hot pot
湖南菜	húnán cài	Hunan cuisine
烤	kǎo	roasted
山东菜	shāndōng cài	Shandong cuisine
四川菜	sìchuān cài	Sichuan cuisine
熏	xūn	smoked
清蒸	qīng zhēng	steamed
卤	lǔ	stew in heavy gravy sauce
炒	chǎo	stir-fry
爆炒	bào chǎo	stir-fry in high heat
浙江菜	zhèjiāng cài	Zhejiang cuisine

cold dishes/starters

卤水拼盘	*lǔ shuǐ pīn pán*	assorted cold marinated meat
酱牛肉	*jiàng niúròu*	braised beef
白切鸡	*bái qiē jī*	cold chicken
盐水鸭肝	*yán shuǐ yāgān*	duck liver in brine
五香熏鱼	*wǔ xiāng xūn yú*	five-spiced fish
香干马兰头	*xiāng gān mǎlántóu*	five-spiced pickled greens
蒜泥白肉	*suàn ní bái ròu*	garlic pork
海蜇拌黄瓜	*hǎizhé bàn huángguā*	jellyfish with cucumber
海带拌粉丝	*hǎidài bàn fěnsī*	seaweed with vermicelli
凉拌笋丝	*liáng bàn sǔnsī*	shredded bamboo shoots
凉拌黄瓜	*liáng bàn huángguā*	shredded cucumber salad
拌土豆丝	*bàn tǔdòu sī*	shredded potato
炝绿豆芽	*qiàng lǜ dòuyá*	bean sprouts salad
小葱拌豆腐	*xiǎo cōng bàn dòufu*	tofu with spring onion

soups

鱼翅汤	*yú chì tāng*	shark's fin soup
三鲜汤	*sān xiān tāng*	'three fresh' soup (meat, prawns and a vegetable)
海米紫菜汤	*hǎimǐ zǐcài tāng*	dried shrimp and seaweed soup
榨菜肉丝汤	*zhàcài ròu sī tāng*	shredded pork and pickled mustard greens soup
酸辣豆腐汤	*suān là dòufu tāng*	hot and sour tofu soup
菠菜粉丝汤	*bōcài fěnsī tāng*	spinach and vermicelli soup
什锦冬瓜汤	*shí jǐn dōngguā tāng*	winter marrow soup
西红柿鸡蛋汤	*xīhóngshì jīdàn tāng*	tomato and egg soup
时菜肉片汤	*shí cài ròu piàn tāng*	sliced pork and seasonal vegetable soup
冬菇肉片汤	*dōnggū ròu piàn tāng*	Chinese mushrooms with sliced pork soup

rice/wheat-based dishes

白米饭	*bái mǐfàn*	boiled rice
蛋炒饭	*dàn chǎo fàn*	egg stir-fried rice
扬州炒饭	*yángzhōu chǎo fàn*	Yangzhou stir-fried rice
粽子	*zòngzi*	glutinous rice wrapped in bamboo leaves
稀饭	*xīfàn*	porridge
锅巴饭	*guōbā fàn*	crispy rice topped with seafood, meat or vegetables
炒年糕	*chǎo nián gāo*	stir-fried rice cake
馒头	*mántou*	steamed buns
花卷	*huājuǎn*	steamed twisted rolls
饼	*bǐng*	pancake
烧饼	*shāobǐng*	with sesame seeds
葱油饼	*cōngyóu bǐng*	with spring onion
馅儿饼	*xiànr bǐng*	with fillings
包子	*bāozi*	steamed filled dumplings
猪肉包子	*zhūròu bāozi*	with pork
叉烧包子	*chāshāo bāozi*	with barbecued pork
牛肉包子	*niúròu bāozi*	with beef
羊肉包子	*yángròu bāozi*	with lamb
三鲜包子	*sān xiān bāozi*	with 'three fresh' (usually meat with seafood)
素包子	*sù bāozi*	with vegetables
豆沙包子	*dòu shā bāozi*	with red-bean paste
小笼包子	*xiǎo lóng bāozi*	small steamed dumplings
饺子	*jiǎozi*	dumplings
锅贴	*guō tiē*	fried dumplings
蒸饺子	*zhēng jiǎozi*	steamed dumplings
素饺子	*sù jiǎozi*	dumplings with vegetable fillings
面/面条	*miàn/miàntiáo*	noodles
炒面	*chǎo miàn*	stir-fried noodles
猪肉丝	*zhū ròu sī*	with shredded pork
豆芽	*dòu yá*	with beansprouts
炸酱面	*zhá jiàng miàn*	noodles with minced meat and soy bean sauce
牛肉面	*niúròu miàn*	noodles with beef
汤面	*tāng miàn*	noodles in soup
馄饨	*hún tun*	won ton
春卷	*chūn juǎn*	spring rolls

pork, beef and lamb dishes

猪肉	zhūròu	pork
粉蒸肉	fěn zhēng ròu	steamed pork with rice
红烧肉	hóng shāo ròu	pork belly braised in soy sauce
回锅肉	huí guō ròu	pork steamed first and then stir-fried with chilli
狮子头	shīzi tóu	'lion's head' (minced pork balls)
蚂蚁上树	mǎyi shàng shù	'ants climbing the tree' (minced pork with vermicelli)
鱼香肉丝	yú xiāng ròu sī	stir-fried shredded pork with chilli, ginger and garlic
糖醋排骨	táng cù páigǔ	sweet and sour spare ribs
木须肉	mùxū ròu	stir-fried sliced pork with eggs
叉烧肉	chāshāo ròu	barbecued pork
辣子肉丁	làzi ròu dīng	stir-fried diced pork with chilli
笋炒肉片	sǔn chǎo ròu piàn	stir-fried sliced pork with bamboo shoots
牛肉	niúròu	beef
五香干煸牛肉丝	wǔ xiāng gān biǎn niúròu sī	deep-fried, shredded beef with five spices
卤/酱牛肉	lǔ/jiàng niúròu	pot-stewed beef in soy sauce
五香牛肉	wǔ xiāng niúròu	stewed beef with five spices
葱爆牛肉丝	cōng bào niúròu sī	shredded beef quick-fried with spring onions
羊肉	yángròu	lamb/mutton
羊肉串	yángròu chuàn	lamb kebabs
涮羊肉	shuàn yángròu	Mongolian lamb hot pot
葱爆羊肉丝	cōng bào yángròu sī	shredded lamb quick-fried with spring onions
羊肉泡馍	yángròu pàomó	braised lamb with pancake

poultry

鸡	jī	chicken
香酥鸡	xiāng sū jī	crispy deep-fried chicken
白斩鸡	bái zhǎn jī	sliced cold chicken
宫保鸡丁	gōng bǎo jī dīng	stir-fried diced chicken with peanuts and chilli

叫花鸡	jiàohuā jī	'beggar's chicken' (marinated chicken)
鸭/鸭子	yā/yāzi	duck
北京烤鸭	běijīng kǎo yā	Beijing roast duck
咸水鸭	xián shuǐ yā	steamed salted duck
香酥鸭	xiāng sū yā	crispy deep-fried duck

fish and seafood dishes

鱼	yú	fish
滑溜鱼片	huáliū yú piàn	stir-fried fish slices with sauce
糖醋鱼块	tángcù yú kuài	sweet and sour fish
清蒸鲤鱼	qīngzhēng lǐyú	steamed carp
红烧鱼	hóngshào yú	fish braised in soy sauce
鱼头炖豆腐	yú tóu dùn dòufu	fish head stewed with tofu
芙蓉虾仁	fúróng xiā rén	stir-fried shrimps coated in egg white
油焖大虾	yóu mèn dà xiā	sautéed king prawns
油焖龙虾	yóu mèn lóng xiā	sautéed lobsters
黄鳝	huáng shàn	farmed eel
炒鳝丝	chǎo shàn sī	stir-fried shredded eel
清蒸螃蟹	qīngzhēng pángxiè	steamed crab
炒鱿鱼	chǎo yóuyú	stir-fried squid
海参	hǎi shēn	sea cucumber

vegetable and tofu dishes

蔬菜	shūcài	vegetable
炒豆芽	chǎo dòu yá	stir-fried bean sprouts
炒时菜	chǎo shí cài	stir-fried seasonal vegetables
冬笋炒扁豆	dōng sǔn chǎo biǎn dòu	stir-fried dwarf beans with bamboo shoots
鲜蘑炒豌豆	xiān mó chǎo wāndòu	stir-fried mushrooms with fresh peas
鱼香茄子	yú xiāng qiézi	aubergines with chilli, ginger and garlic
韭黄炒鸡蛋	jiǔhuáng chǎo jīdàn	stir-fried yellow chives with egg
西红柿炒鸡蛋	xīhóngshì chǎo jīdàn	stir-fried tomato with egg
麻辣豆腐	má là dòufu	tofu with chilli and pepper
砂锅炖豆腐	shāguō dùn dòufu	braised tofu
五香豆腐干	wǔ xiāng dòufu gān	dried tofu with five spices
豆腐丝	dòufu sī	shredded dry tofu sheets

desserts

杏仁豆腐	*xìng rén dòufu*	almond tofu
八宝饭	*bā bǎo fàn*	'eight treasures' (rice pudding with nuts, dates, etc.)
元宵/汤元	*yuánxiāo/tāngyuán*	sweet dumplings made with sticky rice flour
拔丝苹果	*básī píngguǒ*	toffee apple

Chinese-style breakfast

油条	*yóu tiáo*	deep-fried dough sticks
咸菜	*xiáncài*	pickles
稀饭	*xīfàn*	porridge
松花蛋	*sōnghuā dàn*	preserved egg
咸鸭蛋	*xián yādàn*	salted duck egg
小笼包子	*xiǎo lóng bāozi*	small steamed dumplings with fillings
豆浆	*dòu jiāng*	soya milk
馒头	*mántou*	steamed buns

Western-style breakfast

咸肉	*xiánròu*	bacon
煮鸡蛋	*zhǔ jīdàn*	boiled egg
面包	*miànbāo*	bread
黄油	*huángyóu*	butter
咖啡	*kāfēi*	coffee
煎鸡蛋	*jiān jīdàn*	fried egg
果酱	*guǒjiàng*	jam
牛奶	*niúnǎi*	milk
香肠	*xiāngcháng*	sausage
炒鸡蛋	*chǎo jīdàn*	scrambled eggs
糖	*táng*	sugar
烤面包	*kǎo miànbāo*	toast
酸奶	*suānnǎi*	yoghurt

drinks

瓶	*píng*	bottle
啤酒	*píjiǔ*	beer
不含酒精的	*bù hán jiǔjīng de*	alcohol-free
瓶装的	*píngzhuāng de*	bottled
黑啤	*hēipí*	dark
扎啤/鲜啤酒	*zhāpí/xiān píjiǔ*	draught
进口	*jìnkǒu*	imported
当地	*dāngdì*	local
白兰地	*báilándì*	brandy
香槟	*xiāngbīn*	champagne
巧克力（热/冷）	*qiǎokèlì (rè/lěng)*	chocolate (hot/cold)
苹果酒	*píngguǒ jiǔ*	cider
鸡尾酒	*jīwěijiǔ*	cocktail
咖啡	*kāfēi*	coffee
清咖啡	*qīng kāfēi*	black
无咖啡因	*wú kāfēiyīn*	decaffeinated
冰	*bīng*	iced
牛奶咖啡	*niúnǎi kāfēi*	white
加一点奶	*jiā yìdiǎn nǎi*	with a dash of milk
干邑白兰地	*gànyì báilándì*	cognac
金酒及汤力水	*jīnjiǔ jí tānglìshuǐ*	gin and tonic
玻璃杯	*bōli bēi*	glass
冰块儿	*bīngkuàir*	ice
罐儿	*guànr*	jug
… 汁	*… zhī*	… juice
椰子	*yēzi*	coconut
柚子	*yòuzi*	grapefruit
柠檬	*níngméng*	lemon
菠萝	*bōluó*	pineapple
西红柿	*xīhóngshì*	tomato
西瓜	*xīguā*	water melon
鲜榨 …	*xiān zhà …*	freshly squeezed …
黄瓜	*huángguā*	apple
苹果	*píngguǒ*	cucumber
橙子	*chéngzi*	orange
柠檬汁	*níngméngzhī*	lemonade
奶昔	*nǎixī*	milkshake
牛奶（热/凉）	*niúnǎi (rè/liáng)*	milk (hot/cold)
矿泉水	*kuàngquán shuǐ*	mineral water
（带汽/不带汽）	*(dàiqì/bú dàiqì)*	(fizzy/still)

红酒	*hóngjiǔ*	port
朗姆酒	*lǎngmǔjiǔ*	rum
啤酒加雪碧	*píjiǔ jiā xuěbì*	shandy
雪利酒	*xuělìjiǔ*	sherry
苏打水	*sūdǎ shuǐ*	soda
...茶	*... chá*	... tea
红	*hóng*	black
绿	*lǜ*	green
茉莉花	*mòlìhuā*	jasmine
冰	*bīng*	iced
奶	*nǎi*	with milk
汤力水	*tānglìshuǐ*	tonic
伏特加	*fútèjiā*	vodka
葡萄酒	*pútaojiǔ*	wine
干	*gān*	dry
红	*hóng*	red
玫瑰酒	*méiguījiǔ*	rosé
甜	*tián*	sweet
白	*bái*	white
当地葡萄酒	*dāngdì pútaojiǔ*	local wine
威士忌	*wēishìjì*	whisky

Entertainment

what's on

The most popular English language magazine for information on local events and entertainment listings is called 'That's magazine' – 'That's Shanghai', 'That's Beijing' etc. Free copies are available from selected bars, restaurants and most major hotels.

There aren't any tourist information centres in operation in Chinese cities yet. There are many travel agencies which sell one-day tours and can book various tickets. Most large hotels supply tourist information.

festivals

The most important Chinese festival is the Chinese New Year, known as 春节 (*chūn jié*), literally 'Spring Festival', which falls between late January and early February. On the 15th day of the new year is 元宵节 (*yuánxiāo jié*), which is known as the Lantern Festival. 新年好 (*xīn nián hǎo*), meaning 'Happy New Year', can be used for both western New Year and Chinese New Year.

Early to mid September (15 August on the lunar calendar) is 中秋节 (*zhōng qiū jié*), literally 'Mid Autumn Festival', which is also known as the Moon Festival.

what to see

Acrobatic arts The Chinese acrobatic art 杂技 (*zájì*) has existed for more than two thousand years but was frowned upon before 1949. Now it is regarded as an art form, for its combination of graceful movements, harmonious musical accompaniment, tasteful

costumes, and staging. Acrobatic shows are shown regularly in theatres in most big cities.

Peking opera 京剧 (*jīng jù*) is the most famous opera out of the 300 or more types of operas in China. There are performances of traditional opera in virtually every town. The costumes are amazing, and the elaborate stage make-up is fascinating. The performances can be quite noisy.

For a taste of Peking Opera, visit the Lao She Tea House in Beijing, where short episodes of the more famous Peking Operas are performed. The dress code for Chinese opera is very informal.

Music The most popular traditional Chinese musical instruments are:

二胡 (*èrhú*) a two-stringed bowed instrument with a low register, 琵琶 (*pípa*) a plucked string instrument played on one's lap, and 古筝 (*gǔ zhēng*) a plucked string instrument played on a flat surface.

Sport The most popular sports are basketball and table tennis. Football is becoming increasingly popular.

Martial arts It is common to see older people doing Tai Chi and practising martial arts in parks in the early morning.

children

In most places children's tickets are sold according to their height. Normally children under 1 metre 10 centemetres go free, and children above that height have to pay, but with a discount. In some places children under the age of 12 go free.

finding out what's on

you may say ...

I'd like ...	我想要...	wǒ xiǎng yào ...
a city map.	一张市区地图。	yī zhāng shìqū dìtú
an entertainment guide.	一份娱乐指南。	yī fèn yúlè zhǐnán
Do you have any information in English?	有英文的介绍材料吗？	yǒu yīngwén de jièshào cáiliào ma
What is there ... here?	这儿有什么...	zhèr yǒu shénme ...
to see	可看的？	kěkàn de
to do	可做的？	kězuò de
for children	孩子喜欢的？	háizi xǐhuān de
Is there ...	有 ... 吗？	yǒu ... ma
a guided tour?	导游陪同的游览	dǎoyóu péitóng de yóulǎn
a one-day tour to the Great Wall?	长城一日游	chángchéng yī rì yóu
Are there any ...	有...吗？	yǒu ... ma
tennis courts?	网球场	wǎngqiú chǎng
martial art classes?	武术班	wǔ shù bān
Can you recommend...	可以推荐...吗？	kěyǐ tuījiàn ... ma
an interesting museum?	一个有意思的博物馆	yī gè yǒuyìsi de bówùguǎn
a good tea-house?	一家好茶馆	yī jiā hǎo chá guǎn
I'm very interested in ...	我对... 很感兴趣。	wǒ duì ... hěn gǎnxìngqù
pipa.	琵琶	pípa
Tai Chi.	太极拳	tàijíquán
I like Peking Opera (very much).	我(非常)喜欢京剧。	wǒ (fēicháng) xǐhuān jīngjù
This is the film which I like.	这是我喜欢的电影。	zhè shi wǒ xǐhuān de diànyǐng
Which day of the week is the dragon boat race?	星期几有龙舟赛？	xīngqī jǐ yǒu lóng zhōu sài

Entertainment

您喜欢看什么?	*nín xǐhuān kàn shénme*	What do you like to see?
您对什么感兴趣?	*nín duì shénme gǎnxìngqù*	What are you interested in?
今天晚上有... 中国古典音乐会。	*jīntiān wǎnshang yǒu ... zhōngguó gǔdiǎn yīnyuè huì*	There is a ... tonight. classical Chinese music concert
这个星期六有...	*zhè ge xīngqīliù yǒu ...*	There is/are ... this Saturday.
龙舟赛。	*lóng zhōu sài*	dragon boat races
就在那儿。	*jiù zài nàr*	Just over there.

things to do or see

acrobatic show	杂技表演	*zájì biǎoyǎn*
ballet	芭蕾舞	*bālěiwǔ*
circus	马戏表演	*mǎxìbiǎoyǎn*
film	电影	*diànyǐng*
fireworks	焰火	*yànhuǒ*
funfair	游乐活动	*yóulèhuódòng*
horse racing	赛马	*sài mǎ*
opera	歌剧	*gējù*
play/show	戏剧/表演	*xìjù/biǎoyǎn*
Peking Opera	京剧	*jīng jù*
sculpture/painting exhibition	雕塑/绘画展	*diāosù/huìhuà zhǎn*
table-tennis match	乒乓球比赛	*pīngpāngqiú bǐsài*
tennis/football match	网球/足球比赛	*wǎngqiú/zúqiú bǐsài*
traditional dancing	传统舞蹈	*chuántǒng wǔdào*

places to visit

amusement park	游乐场	*yóulè chǎng*
aquarium	海洋馆	*hǎiyáng guǎn*
art gallery	美术馆	*měishù guǎn*
cinema	电影院	*diànyǐngyuàn*
Forbidden City	故宫; 紫禁城	*gù gōng; zǐjìn chéng*
karaoke	卡拉OK歌厅	*kǎlā OK gētīng*
museum	博物馆	*bówùguǎn*
night club	夜总会; 俱乐部	*yè zǒnghuì; jùlèbù*
Summer Palace	颐和园	*yíhé yuán*
(indoor/open air) swimming pool	(室内/室外)游泳池	*(shìnèi/shìwài) yóuyǒng chí*
temple	寺庙	*sìmiào*
Temple of Heaven	天坛	*tiān tán*
Terracotta Army	秦始皇兵马俑	*qínshǐhuáng bīngmǎyǒng*
the Great Wall	长城	*cháng chéng*
theatre	剧院	*jùyuàn*
zoo	动物园	*dòngwùyuán*

getting more information

you may say ...

Where is ...	...在哪儿?	*... zài nǎr*
the concert hall?	音乐厅	*yīnyuè tīng*
Where does the guided tour start?	有导游陪同的游览从哪儿开始?	*yǒu dǎoyóu péitóng de yóulǎn cóng nǎr kāishǐ*
What time does it ...	几点...	*jǐ diǎn ...*
start/finish?	开始/结束?	*kāishǐ/jiéshù*
open/close?	开门/关门?	*kāimén/guānmén*
When does it open?	什么时候开门?	*shénme shíhòu kāimén*
Is it open every day?	每天都开门吗?	*měitiān dōu kāimén ma*
Is it open to the public?	对公众开放吗?	*duì gōngzhòng kāifàng ma*
Do you need tickets?	要买票吗?	*yào mǎi piào ma*
Can you book that for me here?	你能帮我预定吗?	*nǐ néng bāng wǒ yùdìng ma*

Entertainment

you may hear ...

你不用买票。	*nǐ bú yòng mǎi piào*	You don't need tickets.
上午十点到下午六点开门。	*shàngwǔ shí diǎn dào xiàwǔ liù diǎn kāimén*	It's open from 10am till 6pm.
每天都开门。	*měitiān dōu kāimén*	It's open every day.

...不开放。
  星期一
  冬季
	...bù kāifàng
	  xīngqíyī
	  dōngjì
		It's closed ...
		  on Mondays.
		  in winter.

在地图/平面图的这个位置上。	*zài dìtú/píngmiàntú de zhè ge wèizhì shàng*	Here on the map.
在售票处	*zài shòupiào chù*	at the ticket office
上午十点在广场	*shàngwǔ shí diǎn zài guǎngchǎng*	in the main square at 10am

check out 1

You're trying to find out the opening hours of the Forbidden City.

○ 故宫什么时候开门？
gù gōng shénme shíhòu kāimén

– 每天上午八点半 。
měitiān shàngwǔ bā diǎn bàn

○ 几点关门？
jǐ diǎn guānmén

– 下午四点半。
xiàwǔ sì diǎn bàn

Q Which of the following statements is false?
a) The Forbidden City is open at 8:30am.
b) The Forbidden City is closed at 4:30pm.
c) The Forbidden City is closed at 7:30pm.

buying a ticket

you may say ...

Where can I buy tickets?	在哪儿买票？	*zài nǎr mǎi piào*
Do you have any tickets for ...	有…票吗？	*yǒu ... piào ma*
the acrobatic show?	杂技表演的	*zájì biǎoyǎn de*
the Shaoxin Opera?	越剧	*yuè jù*
When exactly tomorrow?	明天什么时候？	*míngtiān shénme shíhòu*
How much is it?	多少钱？	*duō shǎo qián*
Is there a concession for ...	…优惠吗？	*... yōuhuì ma*
students?	学生	*xuéshēng*
senior citizens?	老年人	*lǎonián rén*
people with disabilities?	残障人士	*cánzhàng rénshì*
One adult and two children, please.	买一张成人，两张小孩儿票。	*mǎi yī zhāng chéngrén, liǎng zhāng xiǎoháir piào*
A family ticket, please.	买一张家庭票。	*mǎi yī zhāng jiātíng piào*
Two tickets ... please.	买两张…的票。	*mǎi liǎng zhāng ... de piào*
for Saturday night	星期六晚上	*xīngqīliù wǎnshang*
tomorrow	明天	*míngtiān*
How long does it last?	大概多长时间？	*dàgài duō cháng shíjiān*
Does the film have subtitles in English?	电影有英文字幕吗？	*diànyǐng yǒu yīngwén zìmù ma*
Is there an interval?	中间休息吗？	*zhōngjiān xiūxi ma*
Is it suitable for children?	适合孩子看吗？	*shìhé háizi kàn ma*
Is there wheelchair access?	有残障人士通道吗？	*yǒu cánzhàng rénshì tōngdào ma*
Is this seat taken?	这个座位有人吗？	*zhè ge zuòwèi yǒu rén ma*

Entertainment

...半价。	... bàn jià	Half price for ...
学生	xuéshēng	students.
老人	lǎorén	senior citizens.
就在这儿买票。	jiù zài zhèr mǎi piào	You can buy tickets here.
对不起，（票已经）卖完了。	duìbuqǐ, (piào yǐjīng) mài wán le	Sorry, it's sold out.
今天没有。	jīntiān méi yǒu	There's no show today.
...点开始/结束。	... diǎn kāishǐ/jiéshù	It starts/finishes at ...
演出八点开始。	yǎnchū bā diǎn kāishǐ	The show starts at 8 o'clock.
演三个小时。	yǎn sān ge xiǎoshí	It lasts three hours.
中间休息20分钟。	zhōngjiān xiūxi èrshí fēnzhōng	There's one interval of 20 minutes.
是...	shì ...	It's ...
原声的。	yuán shēng de	in the original language.
配音的。	pèiyīn de	dubbed.
有残障人士通道。	yǒu cánzhàngrénshì tōngdào	There are wheelchair ramps.
可以随便坐。	kěyǐ suíbiàn zuò	You can sit where you like.

signs

存衣间	cúnyījiān	cloakroom
请勿触摸	qǐng wù chùmō	do not touch
入口	rùkǒu	entrance
双号	shuāng hào	even numbers
出口	chūkǒu	exit
问询处	wènxún chù	information desk
女/男	nǚ/nán	ladies/gents
请勿拍照	qǐng wù pāizhào	no photography
单号	dān hào	odd numbers

check out 2

You're buying tickets for an acrobatic show.

○ 今天晚上有杂技表演吗?
  jīntiān wǎnshang yǒu zájì biǎoyǎn ma

– 今天没有,星期六晚上有。
  jīntiān méi yǒu, xīngqīliù wǎnshang yǒu

○ 大概多长时间?
  dàgài duō cháng shíjiān

– 两个半小时。
  liǎng ge bàn xiǎoshí

Q When is the show on?
How long does the show last?

sport

you may say ...

Where can I go ...	可以去哪儿...	*kěyǐ qù nǎr ...*
swimming?	游泳?	*yóuyǒng*
ice skating?	滑冰?	*huá bīng*
Where can we play ...	可以在哪儿打...	*kěyǐ zài nǎr dǎ ...*
table tennis?	乒乓球?	*pīngpāng qiú*
I'd like to learn ...	我想学...	*wǒ xiǎng xué ...*
a martial art.	武术。	*wǔ shù*
Are there any ...	有 ... 吗?	*yǒu ... ma*
martial arts classes?	武术班	*wǔ shù bān*
tennis courts?	网球场	*wǎngqiú chǎng*
I'd like to hire ...	我想租...	*wǒ xiǎng zū ...*
a (tennis) racket.	一副(网球)拍。	*yī fù (wǎngqiú) pāi*
a (mountain) bike.	一辆(山地)自行车。	*yī liàng (shāndi) zixíngchē*

Entertainment

Is it possible to hire a snowboard?	有可能租到滑板吗？	*yǒu kěnéng zūdào huábǎn ma*
How much is it ...	...多少钱？	*... duō shǎo qián*
per hour?	每小时	*měi xiǎoshí*
per day?	每天	*měi tiān*
Is it ...	...吗？	*... ma*
okay for beginners?	适合初学者	*shìhé chūxuézhě*
difficult?	难	*nán*
dangerous?	危险	*wēixiǎn*
Can children do it too?	小孩儿也行吗？	*xiǎoháir yě xíng ma*

you may hear ...

...五十元。	*... wǔshí yuán*	It's 50 yuan ...
一天	*yī tiān*	a day.
一小时	*yī xiǎoshí*	an hour.
你需要...吗？	*nǐ xūyào ... ma*	Do you want ...
上培训班	*shàng péixùnbān*	a lesson?
一位教练	*yī wèi jiàoliàn*	an instructor?
海滩附近有...	*hǎitān fùjìn yǒu...*	There is ... near the beach.
一个网球场。	*yī ge wǎngqiú chǎng*	a tennis court

sports equipment

balls	球	*qiú*
boat	船	*chuán*
golf clubs	高尔夫球棒	*gāoěrfūqiú bàng*
ice skates	冰鞋	*bīng xié*
ski boots	雪靴	*xuē xuē*
skis	雪橇	*xuěqiāo*
snowboard	滑雪板	*huáxuěbǎn*
table-tennis racket	乒乓球拍	*pīngpāngqiú pāi*

swimming

you may say ...

Can I use the hotel pool?	可以使用酒店游泳池吗?	kěyǐ shǐyòng jiǔdiàn yóuyǒng chí ma
Where are ...	...在哪儿?	... zài nǎr
the changing rooms?	更衣室	gèngyī shi
the showers?	淋浴房	linyùfáng
I'd like to hire ...	我想租...	wǒ xiǎng zū...
a towel.	一条毛巾	yī tiáo máojīn
Can we swim here?	我们可以在这儿游泳吗?	wǒmen kěyǐ zài zhèr yóuyǒng ma
Is it safe for children?	对小孩儿安全吗?	duì xiǎohàir ān'quán ma

you may hear ...

你是本店客人吗?	nǐ shi běn diàn kèren ma	Are you staying at this hotel?
对不起，只对本店客人开放。	duìbuqǐ, zhǐ duì běn diàn kèren kāifàng	Sorry, it's only open to guests of the hotel.
不安全。	bù ān'quán	No, it's not safe.

signs

you may see ...

深水区	shēnshuǐ qū	deep
急救	jíjiù	first aid
救生员	jiùshēng yuán	lifeguard
退/涨潮	tuì/zhǎng cháo	low/high tide
请勿在此游泳	qǐng wù zàicǐ yóuyǒng	no swimming here
巨浪危险	jù làng wēixiǎn	strong current

check out 3

You want to take a martial arts lesson.

○ 我想学武术或者太极拳。请问，哪儿有培训班？
wǒ xiǎng xué wǔshù huòzhě tàijíquán. qǐng wèn, nǎr yǒu péixùnbān

– 这儿有武术培训班，没有太极拳培训班。
zhèr yǒu wǔshù péixùnbān, méi yǒu tàijíquán péixùnbān

○ 武术培训班适合初学者吗？
wǔshù péixùnbān shìhé chūxuézhě ma

– 适合。
shìhé

○ 每小时多少钱？
měi xiǎoshí duō shǎo qián

– 两百块。
liǎng bǎi kuài

Q Are there martial art lessons for beginners?
How much is the lesson per hour?

sound check

The sound _c_ is pronounced a bit like 'ts' in 'roasts':

| 从 | _cóng_ | from |
| 在此 | _zài cǐ_ | in here |

practise the following _c_ sounds:

| 残障人士 | _cánzhàng rénshì_ | people with disabilites |
| 存衣间 | _cúnyījiān_ | cloakroom |

try it out

question time

Fill in the blanks with one of the phrases to complete the sentences.

1 京剧 ------ 开始? _jīng jù _____ kāishǐ_
What time does the Peking Opera start?

2 每天十点 ------。 _měi tiān shí diǎn _____
It opens at 10am every day.

3 有 ------ 吗? _yǒu _____ ma_
Does it have English subtitles?

4 大概 ------? _dàgài _____
Roughly how long will it be?

a 开门 _kāimén_
b 几点 _jǐdiǎn_
c 多长时间 _duō cháng shíjiān_
d 英文字幕 _yīngwén zìmù_

match it up

Match the answers to the questions.

1 星期几有龙舟赛？
xīngqī jǐ yǒu lóng zhōu sài

2 多少钱一张京剧票？
duō shǎo qián yī zhāng jīng jù piào

3 电影几点开始？
diàn yǐng jǐ diǎn kāishǐ

a 五十块一张。
wǔshí kuài yī zhāng

b 这个星期六 。
zhè ge xīngqīliù

c 下午三点五十。
xiàwǔ sān diǎn wǔshí

as if you were there

Use the prompts below to ask for information.

(Ask what is there to see here)
您喜欢看什么？
nín xǐhuān kàn shénme

(Say you like Peking Opera very much)
星期六晚上有京剧。
xīngqīliù wǎnshang yǒu jīngjù

(Ask where you can get tickets)
就在这儿买票。
jiù zài zhèr mǎi piào

(Say three tickets please)

linkup

几点开始?	*jǐ diǎn* kāishǐ	**What time does it** start?
故宫什么时候开门?	*gù gōng* **shénme shíhòu** kāimén	**When** does the Forbidden City open?
可以推荐一家好茶馆吗?	*kěyǐ tuījiàn* yī jiā hǎo chá guǎn **ma**	**Can you recommend** a good tea-house?
有英文节目单吗?	**yǒu** yīngwén jiémùdān **ma**	**Do you have** a programme in English?
我（非常）喜欢京剧。	*wǒ (fēicháng) xǐhuān jīng jù*	**I like** Peking Opera (**very much**).
我想学武术。	*wǒ xiǎng xué wǔ shù*	**I'd like** to learn a martial art.
可以去哪儿游泳?	*kěyǐ qù nǎr* yóuyǒng	**Where can I go** swimming?

am and pm

There are no specific terms for am or pm. They are indicated by putting the word for:

morning 早上 *zǎoshang* (or 上午 *shàngwǔ*)

afternoon 下午 *xiàwǔ*

or evening 晚上 *wǎnshang* in front of the time.

早上/上午八点	*zǎoshang/shàngwǔ bā diǎn*	8am
下午三点	*xiàwǔ sān diǎn*	3pm
晚上七点	*wǎnshang qī diǎn*	7pm

time expressions

Precise times such as '3 o'clock' come immediately before the verb:

京剧	晚上	七点	开始。
jīng jù	*wǎnshang*	*qī diǎn*	*kāishǐ*
Lit. Peking Opera	evening	7 o'clock	start

The Peking Opera starts at 7pm.

Other time expressions such as 'this Saturday' or 'this morning' can be placed either just before the verb, or at the beginning of the sentence:

每个星期一	有	杂技表演。
měi ge xīngqīyī	*yǒu*	*zájì biǎoyǎn*
Lit. every Monday	have	acrobatic show

There are acrobatic shows every Monday.

Emergencies

reporting crime

There are two types of police: 人民警察 (*rénmín jǐngchá*) 'People's Police', who deal with petty and serious crimes, and 交通警察 (*jiāotōng jǐngchá*) the traffic police, who maintain traffic incidents. Look out for the sign for police station: 公安局 (*gōng'ān jú*).

health

Chemists are generally open from 8am to 8pm. Most chemists sell both Western medicine and Chinese medicine, but some only sell Chinese medicine. For western medicine, only non-prescription medicines are sold at chemists. Prescribed medicines can only be obtained from hospital pharmacies.

If you need to see a doctor, go to a hospital. An appointment is not required. At the hospital go to the registration window 挂号 (*guàhào*). You'll have to pay the consultation fee up front, and then you'll be given a number.

You may not have the privacy that you are used to, as in most hospitals two doctors share one consultation room. The hospital's emergency service operates 24 hours a day.

Traditional Chinese medicine TCM is called 中医 (*zhōngyī*), it incorporates not only herbal preparations, but also treatment methods such as acupuncture. When consulting a TCM doctor (also called *zhōngyī*), your pulse will be taken, and you will be aksed questions about your health.

travellers with disabilities

The facilities for travellers with disabilities are very limited, although they have been improving in recent years. In Beijing and Shanghai, all pedestrian crossings play a beeping sound for the visually impaired.

telephones

Mobile phones are widely used in China. You can buy a pay-as-you-go SIM card to use in your own handset. Make sure that the SIM card you buy only charges you for making calls (some SIM cards also charge for receiving calls).

Public phones are easy to find. Some are inside shops, you pay after you make the call. Others only take IC (integrated circuit) cards which allow you to make both international and domestic calls.

useful phone numbers

Police 110
Fire 119
Traffic accident 122
Ambulance 120
Beijing Red Cross First Aid Centre 999

emergency phrases

you may say ...

Help!	救命; 救救我!	*jiùming; jiùjiu wǒ*
Excuse me!	对不起!; 劳驾!	*duìbuqǐ; láo jià*
Can you help me?	你能帮助我吗?	*nǐ néng bāngzhù wǒ ma*
Does anyone speak English?	有人讲英语吗?	*yǒu rén jiǎng yīngyǔ ma*
There's been an accident.	出事故了。	*chū shìgù le*
We need a doctor.	得找个医生。	*děi zhǎo ge yīshēng*
It's urgent!	情况紧急!	*qíngkuàng jǐnjí*
Don't move ...	别动 ...	*bié dòng ...*
me.	我。	*wǒ*
him/her.	他/她。	*tā*
Where's ...	...在哪儿?	*... zài nǎr*
the police station?	公安局	*gōng'ān jú*
the Red Cross First Aid Centre?	红十字急救中心	*hóng shízì jíjiù zhōngxīn*
Where do I get a registration number?	在哪儿挂号?	*zài nǎr guàhào*
I need ...	我需要...	*wǒ xūyào ...*
to see a doctor.	看医生。	*kàn yīshēng*
an ambulance.	一辆救护车。	*yī liàng jiùhùchē*
to report a crime.	检举一起案子。	*jiǎnjǔ yī qǐ ànzi*
Where's the nearest...	离这儿最近的... 在哪儿?	*lí zhèr zuìjìn de ...zài nǎr*
hospital?	医院	*yīyuàn*
chemist?	药店	*yàodiàn*
public phone?	公用电话	*gōngyòng diànhuà*
Leave me alone.	别管我。	*bié guǎn wǒ*
I'll call the police.	我要打电话叫警察。	*wǒ yào dǎ diànhuà jiào jǐngchá*

Emergencies

telling the doctor or dentist

you may say ...

I'd like an appointment with ...	我想预约...	wǒ xiǎng yùyuē ...
a doctor.	一位医生。	yī wèi yīshēng
a dentist.	一位牙医。	yī wèi yáyī
I've got ...	我....	wǒ ...
a headache.	头疼。	tóuténg
toothache.	牙疼。	yáténg
stomach ache.	胃疼。	wèiténg
I've got ...	我...	wǒ ...
a cold.	感冒了。	gǎnmào le
flu.	得了流感。	de le liúgǎn
a rash.	出疹子了。	chū zhěnzi le
diarrhoea.	拉肚子。	lādùzi
It hurts here.	这儿疼。	zhèr téng
My ... hurts (a lot).	我...疼（得厉害）。	wǒ ... téng (de lìhai)
stomach	肚子	dùzi
I have a bad cough.	我咳嗽得厉害。	wǒ késòu de lìhài
I'm constipated.	我便秘。	wǒ biànmì
My child has a temperature.	我的孩子发烧了。	wǒde háizi fā shāo le
She/He feels ...	她/他...	tā ...
sick.	病了。	bìng le
dizzy.	头晕。	tóuyūn
I'm allergic to ...	我对...过敏。	wǒ duì ... guòmǐn
antibiotics.	抗生素	kàngshēngsù
aspirin.	阿司匹林	āsīpǐlín
I'm ...	我...	wǒ ...
diabetic.	有糖尿病。	yǒu tángniàobìng
epileptic.	有癫痫病。	yǒu diānxiánbìng
HIV positive.	是艾滋病病毒携带者。	shì àizībìng bìngdú xiédàizhě
pregnant.	怀孕了	huáiyùn le
I have ...	我患有...。	wǒ huàn yǒu ...
asthma.	哮喘	xiàochuǎn
high/low blood pressure.	高/低血压	gāo/dī xuěyā

I've ... myself.	我把自己...了。	*wǒ bǎ zìjǐ ... le*
cut	划破	*huàpò*
burnt	烫伤	*tàngshāng*
I've been ...	我被...了。	*wǒ bèi ...*
bitten.	咬了。	*yǎo le*
stung.	蜇了。	*zhē le*
I can't ...	我不能...了。	*wǒ bù néng ...le*
breathe properly.	正常呼吸	*zhèngcháng hūxī*
move.	动	*dòng*
I have a broken tooth.	我的一个牙断了。	*wǒde yī ge yá duàn le*
I've lost ...	...不见了。	*... bú jiàn le*
a filling.	填充物	*tián chōngwù*
a crown.	牙冠	*yáguān*

you may hear ...

哪儿不舒服？	*nǎr bù shūfu*	What's wrong with you?
这儿疼吗？	*zhèr téng ma*	Does it hurt here?
哪儿疼？	*nǎr téng*	Where does it hurt?
...疼吗？	*... téng ma*	Does your ... hurt?
嗓子	*sǎngzi*	throat
吃什么药了吗？	*chī shénme yào le ma*	Are you on medication?
你对什么过敏吗？	*nǐ duì shenme guòmǐn ma*	Are you allergic to anything?
不太严重。	*bù tài yánzhòng*	It isn't serious.
是...	*shì ...*	It's ...
扭伤。	*niǔshāng*	a sprain.
骨折。	*gǔzhé*	a fracture.
食物中毒。	*shíwù zhòngdú*	food poisoning.
你需要...	*nǐ xūyào...*	You need ...
做手术。	*zuò shǒushù*	an operation.
住院。	*zhù yuàn*	to go to hospital.
拍x光片。	*pāi X guāng piàn*	an X-ray.
我需要血样。	*wó xūyào xuě yàng*	I need a blood sample.

你必须…	*nǐ bìxū…*	You must …
休息。	*xiūxí*	rest.
多喝水。	*duō hē shuǐ*	drink lots of water.
千万不要…	*qiānwàn bú yào…*	You mustn't …
喝酒。	*hē jiǔ*	drink alcohol.
我给你放点儿（临时）填充物。	*wǒ gěi nǐ fàng diǎnr (línshí) tiánchōngwù*	I'll put a (temporary) filling in.
这颗牙必须拔掉。	*zhè kē yá bìxū bá diào*	I'll have to take the tooth out.
这是处方。	*zhè shì chǔfāng*	Here's a prescription.

check out 1

You're explaining your symptoms to the doctor.

- ○ 哪儿不舒服？
  nǎr bù shūfu

- – 我拉肚子。
  wǒ lā dùzi

- ○ 肚子疼吗？
  dùzi téng ma

- – 很疼。
  hěn téng

Q   You've got diarrhoea: true or false?

at the chemist's

you may say ...

I'd like something ...	我想买一点儿...的药。	wǒ xiǎng mǎi yī diǎnr ... de yào
for sea sickness.	预防晕船	yùfáng yūn chuán
for insect stings.	治蚊虫叮咬	zhì wénchóng dīngyǎo
for sunburn.	治太阳灼伤	zhì tàiyáng zhuóshāng
Do you have any ...	有没有...?	yǒu méi yǒu ...
after-sun lotion?	晒后修复液	shàihòu xiūfùyè
aspirin?	阿司匹林	āsīpǐlín
cough mixture?	止咳液	zhǐkéyè
contact lens solution?	隐形眼镜护理液	yǐnxíng yǎnjìng hùlǐyè
I need some ...	我想买点儿...	wǒ xiǎng mǎi diǎnr ...
antihistamine.	止痒药/治花粉病的药。	zhǐyǎng yào/zhì huāfěnbìng de yào
mosquito repellent.	驱蚊液。	qūwén yè
plasters.	膏药。	gāoyào
cold medicine.	感冒药。	gǎnmàoyào
Do you have anything for... ?	有没有什么药可以治...?	yǒu méi yǒu shénme yào kěyǐ zhì ...
a sore throat.	喉咙肿痛	hóulóng zhǒngtòng
diarrhoea.	拉肚子	lādùzi
I've got ...	我...	wǒ ...
hayfever.	有花粉病。	yǒu huāfěnbìng
an upset stomach.	肚子不舒服。	dùzi bù shūfu
How do I take it/them?	这种药怎么吃?	zhè zhǒng yào zěnme chī

Emergencies

you may hear ...

你正在服用其它药物吗?	nǐ zhèngzài fúyòng qítā yàowù ma	Are you taking any other medicine?
吃...	chī ...	Take ...
这些药片。	zhèxiē yàopiàn	these tablets.
涂抹...	túmǒ ...	Apply ...
这种药水	zhèzhǒng yàoshuǐ	this lotion.
...吃。	... chī	Take ....
饭前	fàn qián	before meals.
饭后	fàn hòu	after meals.
空腹	kōngfù	on an empty stomach.
用水服下	yòng shuǐ fú xià	Take with water.
每次一勺	měi cì yī sháo	one spoonful
每天两次	měitiān liǎng cì	twice a day
吞服	tūn fú	Swallow whole.
会引起头晕或打瞌睡。	huì yǐnqǐ tóuyūn huò dǎ kēshuì	May cause drowsiness.

check out 2

You go to the chemist to ask for medicine and advice.

○ 有没有止咳液?
  yǒu méi yǒu zhǐkéyè

– 有。给你。
  yǒu. gěi nǐ

○ 这种药有副作用吗?
  zhè zhǒng yào yǒu fù zuòyòng ma

– 有饭前吃。
  yǒu fàn qián chī

Q What medicine do you ask for?
What advice have you been given?

traditional Chinese medicine

you may say ...

I'd like to see a TCM doctor.	我想看中医。	*wǒ xiǎng kàn zhōngyī*

I'd like to try ...
  some TCM.
  acupuncture.
	我想试试...
	  中药。
	  针灸。
		wǒ xiǎng shìshi ...
		  zhōng yào
		  zhēnjiǔ

Do you do TCM foot massage?	你们有中医足疗吗？	*nǐmen yǒu zhōngyī zú liáo ma*
Are there side effects?	有副作用吗？	*yǒu fùzuòyòng ma*

you may hear ...

你想吃中药还是西药？	*nǐ xiǎng chī zhōngyào háishì xī yào*	Would you like TCM or Western medicine?
我号一下你的脉，好吗？	*wǒ hào yīxià nǐde mài, hǎo ma*	May I feel your pulse?
请把舌头伸出来。	*qǐng bǎ shétou shēn chūlái*	Can you stick out your tongue please?
你在吃其它药物吗？	*nǐ zài chī qítā yàowù ma*	Are you taking any other medicine?
给你一些感冒冲剂。	*gěi nǐ yìxiē gǎnmào chōngjì*	Here are some cold relief sachets.

parts of the body

arm	胳膊	*gēbo*
back	背	*bèi*
chest	胸	*xiōng*
ear	耳朵	*ěrduo*
eye/eyes	眼睛	*yǎnjīng*
finger	手指	*shǒuzhǐ*
foot	脚	*jiǎo*
hand	手	*shǒu*
head	头	*tóu*
hips	臀部	*túnbù*
kidneys	肾	*shèn*

knee	膝盖	*xīgài*
leg	腿	*tuǐ*
lung	肺	*fèi*
mouth	嘴	*zuǐ*
neck	颈	*jǐng*
nose	鼻子	*bízi*
shoulders	肩	*jiān*
stomach	胃	*wèi*
tooth/teeth	牙	*yá*
throat	嗓子; 喉咙	*sǎngzi; hóulóng*

at the police station

you may say ...

I've lost my ...	我的...丢了。	*wǒde ... diū le*
wallet.	钱包	*qiánbāo*
passport.	护照	*hùzhào*
daughter.	女儿	*nǚ'ér*
My ... was stolen.	我的...被偷了。	*wǒde ... bèi tōu le*
watch	表	*biǎo*
handbag	包	*bāo*
It was ...	是...	*shì ...*
big.	大的。	*dà de*
black.	黑色的。	*hēisè de*
made of leather.	皮的。	*pí de*
I've been ...	我被 ...了。	*wǒ bèi ... le*
attacked.	打	*dǎ*
mugged.	抢	*qiǎng*
yesterday ...	昨天 ...	*zuótiān ...*
morning	早上	*zǎoshang*
afternoon	下午	*xiàwǔ*
evening	晚上	*wǎnshang*
this morning	今天早上	*jīntiān zǎoshang*
in ...	在...	*zài ...*
a shop	一家商店	*yī jiā shāngdiàn*
the street	路上	*lùshàng*

you may hear ...

什么颜色的?	shénme yánsè de	What colour is it?
什么样的?	shénmeyàng de	What is it like?
里面有什么?	lǐmiàn yǒu shénme	What was in it?
什么时候?	shénme shíhòu	When?
在哪儿丢的?	zài nǎr diū de	Where did you lose it?
你受伤了吗?	nǐ shòushāng le ma	Are you hurt?
你的... 是什么?	nǐde ... shì shénme	What's your ...
名字	míngzi	name?
住址	zhùzhǐ	address?
请出示护照。	qǐng chūshì hùzhào	Your passport, please.
填一下这个表格。	tián yī xià zhè ge biǎogé	Fill in this form.
... 再来一趟。	... zài lái yītàng	Come back ...
随后	suíhòu	later.
明天	míngtiān	tomorrow.
你得付罚款。	nǐ děi fù fákuǎn	You have to pay a fine.

valuables

briefcase	公文包	gōngwénbāo
camcorder	摄像机	shèxiàngjī
(digital) camera	(数码)相机	(shùmǎ) xiàngjī
credit card	信用卡	xìnyòng kǎ
driving licence	驾驶执照	jiàshǐ zhízhào
handbag	手提包	shǒutíbāo

jewellery	首饰	*shǒushi*
keys	钥匙	*yàoshi*
necklace	项链	*xiàngliàn*
laptop	手提电脑	*shǒutí diànnǎo*
mobile phone	手机	*shǒujī*
money	钱	*qián*
MP3-player	MP3（播放器）	*MP3 (bōfàngqì)*
passport	护照	*hùzhào*
purse	钱夹	*qiánjiā*
ring	戒指	*jièzhǐ*
rucksack	背包	*bēibāo*
suitcase	旅行箱	*lǚxingxiāng*
tickets	票	*piào*
traveller's cheques	旅行支票	*lǚxíng zhīpiào*
wallet	钱包	*qiánbāo*
watch	表	*biǎo*

check out 3

You report a theft to the police.

○ 我的手提包被偷了。
wǒde shǒutíbāo bèi tōu le

– 什么颜色的?
shénme yánsè de

○ 黑色。
hēisè

– 里面有什么?
lǐmiàn yǒu shénme

○ 护照和手机。
hùzhào hé shǒujī

Q
What was stolen?
What colour is it?
What was in it?

car breakdown

I've broken down.	我的车抛锚了。	*wǒ de chēpāomáo le*
I had an accident.	我出车祸了。	*wǒ chū chē huò le*
... isn't/aren't working.	... 坏了。	*... huài le*
The brakes aren't working.	刹车坏了。	*chāchē huài le*
It won't start.	发动不起来。	*fā dòng bù qǐlái*
I've got a flat tyre.	车胎瘪了。	*chētāi biě le*
I've run out of petrol.	没油了。	*méi yóu le*
Could you send a mechanic?	能派一位修理工吗？	*néng pài yī wèi xiūlǐgōng ma*
When will it be ready?	什么时候能修好？	*shénme shíhòu néng xiū hǎo*

毛病在哪儿？	*máobing zài nǎr*	What's wrong?
你在什么地方？	*nǐ zài shénme difang*	Where are you?
你的车牌号是多少？	*nǐ de chēpái hào shì duō shǎo*	What's your registration number?
...能修好。	*... néng xiū hǎo*	It will be ready ...
一小时后	*yī xiǎoshí hòu*	in an hour.
星期一	*xīngqīyī*	on Monday.

car parts

accelerator	油门	*yóumén*
battery	电池	*diànchí*
bonnet	引擎盖	*yǐnqíng gài*
brakes	刹车	*shāchē*
bumper	保险杠	*bǎoxiǎngàng*
clutch	挡	*dǎng*
exhaust pipe	排气管	*páiqì guǎn*
fan belt	风扇皮带	*fēngshàn pídài*

gearbox	变速器	*biànsù qi*
headlights	前灯	*qián dēng*
radiator	暖气	*nuǎnqì*
spark plug	火花塞	*huǒhuā sāi*
steering wheel	方向盘	*fāngxiàng pàn*
windscreen	挡风玻璃	*dǎngfēng bōli*

bicycle parts

back light	后灯	*hòu dēng*
chain	链条	*liàntiáo*
frame	框架	*kuāngjià*
front light	前灯	*qián dēng*
gears	变速器	*biànsùqí*
handlebars	扶手	*fú shǒu*
inner tube	内带	*nèi dài*
pump	气筒	*qìtǒng*
saddle	车座	*chēzuò*
spokes	车轮辐条	*chēlún fútiáo*
tyre	轮胎	*lúntāi*
valve	气门芯	*qìménxīn*
wheel	车轮子	*chēlúnzi*
wheel rim	轮子边缘	*lún zi biānyuán*

sound check

The sound z is a bit like 'ds' in 'loads':

再见	*zài jiàn*	goodbye
在哪儿	*zài nǎr*	where is ...

Practise the following words with the z sound:

做手术	*zuò shǒushù*	to have an operation
足疗	*zú liáo*	foot massage
红十字	*hóng shízì*	red cross

try it out

picture this

Match the pictures to the words.

1   **2**

3   **4**

a	表	*biǎo*
b	止咳液	*zhǐkéyè*
c	手提包	*shǒutíbāo*
d	药片	*yàopiàn*

what do you need?

Sort your holiday packing into the following groups:

a personal
b work
c travel essentials

1	信用卡	*xìnyòng kǎ*
2	项链	*xiàngliàn*
3	护照	*hùzhào*
4	钱包	*qiánbāo*
5	相机	*xiàngjī*
6	手提电脑	*shǒutí diànnǎo*
7	戒指	*jièzhǐ*
8	公文包	*gōngwénbāo*
9	手机	*shǒujī*

as if you were there

You're at the chemist's. Follow the prompts below to get what you need.

(*Tell the chemist that you have got a cold*)
你想吃中药还是西药？
nǐ xiǎng chī zhōngyào háishì xī yào

(*Say you'd like to try some traditional Chinese medicine*)
好的。给你一些感冒冲剂。
hǎode. gěi nǐ yīxiē gǎnmào chōngjì

(*Ask how to take them*)
每天两次，饭前吃。
měitiān liǎng cì, fàn qián chī

linkup

key phrases

你能帮助我吗?	*nǐ néng* bāngzhù wǒ *ma*	**Can you** help me?
我需要看医生。	*wǒ xūyào* kàn yīshēng	**I need** to see a doctor.
我嗓子疼。	*wǒ* sǎngzi *téng*	**My** throat **hurts.**
我头疼。	*wǒ* tóu *téng*	I have a head**ache.**
有没有止咳液?	*yǒu méi yǒu* zhǐkéyè	**Do you have** any cough mixture?
这种药怎么吃?	zhè zhǒng yào *zěnme chī*	**How do I take** it/them?
我的护照被偷了。	*wǒde* hùzhào *bèi tōu le*	My passport **was stolen.**
我的钱包丢了。	*wǒde* qiánbāo *diū le*	**I've lost** my wallet.

possession

To indicate that something belongs to somebody add 的 *de* to the personal pronoun ('I', 'you', 'he', 'she' etc):

我 *wǒ* I/me   becomes   我的 *wǒde* my/mine

我的钱包丢了。   *wǒde qiánbāo diū le*   I've lost my wallet.
那个钱包是我的。   *nà ge qiánbāo shì wǒde*   That wallet is mine.

的 *de* often gets omitted when talking about close family members or parts of the body:

我嗓子疼。   *wǒ sǎngzi téng*   My throat hurts.

missing words

Pronouns are often omitted if the context makes it clear what or who is being discussed:

(你)有没有止咳液？
(nǐ) yǒu méi yǒu zhǐkéyè
Do you have any cough mixture?

这种药(我)怎么吃？
zhè zhǒng yào (wǒ) zěnme chī
How do I take it/them?

In the examples above the words for 'you' 你 *nǐ* , and 'I' 我 *wǒ* can be left out.

For more on pronouns see the Language Builder, p132. ·····⫶

past tense

Add 了 *le* after a verb, or at the end of the sentence to indicate that something happened or has taken place:

我的钱包丢了。
wǒde qiánbāo diū le
I've lost my wallet.

Doing **Business**

protocol

Titles are important in Chinese business circles. Job titles such as 'manager' and 'director' are used as forms of address as well as forms of reference. For example, if someone's surname is 张 (*zhāng*) and they are a manager, they will be referred to as 张经理 (*zhāng jīnglǐ*) literally Zhang manager, and will be addressed in the same way.

When you meet your business partners for the first time, always dress formally, and be prepared to exchange business cards after shaking hands. It's useful to have your business cards printed in both Roman script and Chinese characters.

Business hours in China are normally from 8am to 5pm, usually with a two-hour lunch break.

gifts & giving

Gift-giving is very important. Gifts are usually exchanged at the end of a meeting or banquet.
(see p7 for inappropriate gifts)

business entertaining

Eating out is still the main form of business entertaining. Business lunches and dinners are often elaborate affairs, consisting of at least a dozen dishes. Most restaurants have private rooms, often with karaoke equipment.

To show their hospitality, Chinese people like to toast their guests. They will say 干杯 (*gānbēi*) to you first, and then expect you to finish your drink. If you don't drink alcohol, it is advisable to inform your host before the meal, to avoid embarrassment.

women in business

There are more and more women holding middle to senior management positions. You can either use their titles to address them, or use 小姐 (*xiǎojie*) to address a young woman and 女士 (*nǚshì*) to address a middle-aged or an older woman.

useful phrases

you may say ...

I've come for the three o'clock meeting.	我前来出席三点的会议。	*wǒ qiánlái chūxí sān diǎn de huìyì*
My name's	我叫...	*wǒ jiào...*
May I have your surname?	您贵姓?	*nín guì xìng*
I'm pleased to meet you.	见到您很高兴。	*jiàndào nín hěn gāoxìng*
I look forward to doing business with you.	希望能够与您在生意方面合作。	*xīwàng nénggòu yǔ nín zài shēngyì fāngmiàn hézuò*
This is a gift from ... my hometown. my company.	这是...的礼物。 我家乡 我们公司	*zhè shì... de lǐwù wǒ jiāxiāng wǒmen gōngsī*
Thank you very much. I'm pleased to receive this.	非常感谢。我很高兴接受这一馈赠。	*fēicháng gǎnxiè. wǒ hěn gāoxing jiēshòu zhè yī kuìzèng*
Here is/are the document(s) for the meeting.	这是会议文件。	*zhè shì huìyì wénjiàn*
I'd be grateful if you would read this/that.	如果您能把这个/那个读一下，我将非常感谢。	*rúguǒ nín néng bǎ zhège/nàge dú yīxià, wǒ jiāng fēicháng gǎnxiè*
Thank you very much for your hospitality today.	非常感谢您今天的盛情款待。	*fēicháng gǎnxiè nín jīntiān de shèngqíng kuǎndài*
Sorry, I don't drink alcohol.	对不起，我不会喝酒。	*duìbuqǐ, wǒ bú huì hē jiǔ*
Not at all, it's my pleasure.	没什么，这是应该的。	*méi shénme, zhè shì yīnggāi de*
I look forward to continuing our business relationship.	希望我们 (今后)能够继续合作。	*xīwàng wǒmen (jīnhòu) nénggòu jìxù hézuò*
Thank you for your hard work today.	谢谢您，今天辛苦了。	*xièxie nín, jīntiān xīnkǔ le*

Doing **Business**

you may say ...

you may say ...

不好意思，让您久等了。	bùhǎoyìsi, ràng nín jiǔ děng le	Very sorry to have kept you waiting.
哪里，哪里。	nǎli, nǎli	Not at all (as a response to a compliment).
过奖。	guòjiǎng	I'm flattered (as a response to a compliment).
这是我们的一点儿心意。	zhè shì wǒmen de yīdiǎnr xīnyì	This is a very small present.
谢谢你的礼物。	xièxie nǐde lǐwù	Thank you for your present.
我会珍惜它的。	wǒ huì zhēnxī tā de	I will treasure it.
别客气，咱们是老朋友了。	bié kèqi, zánmen shì lǎo péngyou le	No need to be polite, we are old friends.
我想请你出去吃饭。	wǒ xiǎng qǐng nǐ chūqu chīfàn	I'd like to take you out for a meal.
我请客。	wǒ qǐngkè	It's my treat.
干杯!	gānbēi	Cheers!
祝合作成功。	zhù hézuò chénggōng	Wishing our cooperation a success.

useful words

CEO	总裁	zǒng cái
chairman	主席	zhǔxí
chief engineer	总工程师	zǒng gōngchéngshī
deputy manager	副经理	fù jīnglǐ
director	主任	zhǔrèn
manager	经理	jīnglǐ
manager (factory)	厂长	chǎngzhǎng
managing director	总经理	zǒng jīnglǐ

measure words

In English, only certain nouns are modified by this category of words. For example 'slice' in 'a slice of bread', 'pair' in 'a pair of glasses', etc. Every noun in Chinese, when preceded by a number or a demonstrative pronoun (eg 'this', 'that') must have a measure word. Different measure words are used with different nouns. For example, *zhāng* is used in *yī zhāng dìtú* 'one map', *liàng* is used in *sān liàng chē* 'three cars'. Below are some of the most commonly used measure words:

character	pinyin	category	examples
包	*bāo*	parcel, packet	books, biscuits
杯	*bēi*	cup, glass	coffee, beer
本	*běn*	volume	dictionary
个	*gè*	people	man, girl
家	*jiā*	organisation	hotel
块	*kuài*	square piece	soap
辆	*liàng*	things with wheels	bike, car
瓶	*píng*	bottle, jar	beer, jam
条	*tiáo*	long and winding	scarf
头	*tóu*	big animals	cow
张	*zhāng*	thin, flat	paper
只	*zhī*	small animals	chicken
座	*zuò*	solid	building

If in doubt which one to use, the measure word *gè*, usually pronounced with a neutral tone, can be used in most circumstances. There are some exceptions. Measure words are not used in front of *tiān* 'day' and and *nián* 'year', eg:

> *sān tiān*   three days
>
> *yī nián*   one year

Language **Builder**

nouns

Nouns in Chinese have no singular and plural distinctions:

yī zhāng **dìtú**   one map
sān zhāng **dìtú** three maps

articles

There are no articles ('a', 'an', 'the') in Chinese. *Wǒ qù mǎi* **dìtú** can mean 'I'm going to buy a map' or 'I'm going to buy the map'. The context and measure word used will help to clarify the meaning.

yī one + measure word
zhè/nà (this/that) + measure word

verbs

Verbs have only one form. For example, *qù* means 'to go to':

Wǒ **qù** *Zhōngguó.*   I go to China.
Tā **qù** *Zhōngguó.*   He/She goes to China.
Wǒmen **qù** *Zhōngguó.*   We go to China.

Verbs do not change their forms to indicate past, present, future or continuous.

- The past can be indicated by the particle *le* which is placed after the verb or at the end of the sentence:

  Tā qù **le** *Zhōngguó.*   He/She has gone to China.
  or
  He/She went to China.

- If you want to say that you have experienced something or you have been somewhere, place the particle *quò* straight after the verb:

  Tā chī **quò** *Zhōngguó fàn.*   He/She has had Chinese food.

- If you want to indicate where, when and how something happened in the past, place the particle *de* after the verb or at the end of the sentence:

	Wǒ	*zuótiān*	*dào* **de**		*Běijīng.*
Lit.	I	yesterday	arrived in		Beijing.

I arrived in Beijing yesterday.

Very often, *shì* (to be) is used with *de* to signal emphasis:

Wǒ **shì** *zuótiān* *dào* **de** *Běijīng.*

It was yesterday that I arrived in Beijing.

- However, the above particles are normally not used with static verbs such as *shì* (to be), *yǒu* (to have), *zhīdào* (to know), *xiāngxìn* (to believe), etc. In these cases knowing whether the verbs are in the present or past tense depends on time expressions and the context:

	Sān nián qián	*tā*	**shì**	*lǎoshī.*
Lit.	Three years ago he		be	teacher.

He was a teacher three years ago.

The future tense is usually indicated by time phrases or by placing particles such as *jiāng* (shall), *yào* (will) before the verb:

	Wǒ	**míngnián**	*qù Zhōngguó.*
Lit.	I	next year	go China.

I'm going to China next year.

Wǒ **yào** *qù Zhōngguó.*   I will be going to China.

- The continuous tense is indicated by the continuous particle *zài* or *zhèngzài*, which is placed before the verb:

Wǒ **zài** *kàn diànshì.*   I am watching TV.

The above sentence can also mean 'I was watching TV' when in the right context.

Language **Builder**

adjectives and adverbs

Adjectives (describing words) are placed before nouns, for example, *hǎo dìfang* 'good place'. Note that *de* is inserted between an adjective and a noun if:

- an adverb is placed before an adjective:

  hěn hǎo **de** dìfang   very good place

- the adjective used consists of two syllables:

  piàoliang de dìfang   beautiful place

Descriptive adjectives come before the noun:

    xiǎo fángjiān   small room
    rè shuǐ   hot water

These words can also be put after the noun to explain or describe the noun/noun phrase, and in these cases they have an additional meaning of 'to be'. So you don't need to use the verb *shì* (to be):

    Nǐde fángjiān **xiǎo**.   Your room is small.
    Zhè ge fángjiān tài **rè**.   This room is too hot.

These type of words, when used after the noun, are usually modified by adverbs such as *hěn* (very), *tǐng* (rather), *tài* (too), etc:

    Nǐde fángjiān **hěn** xiǎo.   Your room is very small.

pronouns

The following personal pronouns in Chinese can be used in both the subject position and the object position:

wǒ	I, me
nǐ	you (singular)
nín	you (polite form)
tā	he/she, him/her, it
wǒmen	we, us
nǐmen	you (plural)
tāmen	they, them

For example:

Wǒ ài tā	I love her/him.
Tā ài wǒ	He/She loves me.

Adding de to the personal pronouns forms the possessive:

wǒde	my/mine
nǐde	your/yours (singular)
tāde	his/his
tāde	her/hers
wǒmende	our/ours
nǐmende	your/yours (plural)
tāmende	their/theirs

de often gets omitted in front of close family members or parts of the body:

Wǒ māma shì lǎoshī.	My mother is a teacher.
Wǒ sǎngzi téng.	My throat hurts.

The pronoun 'it' is seldomly used in Chinese, and tends to get omitted when it follows a verb:

Wǒ xǐhuān.	I like it.

Language **Builder**

Pronouns such as 'you', 'I', 'this', etc. are often omitted if the context makes it clear what or who is under discussion. For example, the pronouns in brackets below are often omitted:

(Nǐ) néng bāngbang máng ma. Can you help?

(Zhège) yǒu fù zuòyòng ma. Does this have side effects?

negation

When you negate a sentence in English, you put 'do not', 'does not', 'did not', etc. before the verb. In Chinese, you simply put the negation word before the verb. The two main negation words are: *bù* and *méi*.

bù is used in most sentences. For example:

	Tā	*bù*	*xǐhuān*	*Zhōngguó fàn.*
Lit.	He	not	like	China food.

(He doesn't like Chinese food.)

Méi is used to negate the verb *yǒu* (to have); and to indicate when something has not happened or did not happen.

	Wǒ	*méi*	*yǒu*	*Zhōngguó chá.*
Lit.	I	not	have	China tea.

(I don't have Chinese tea.)

	Tā	*méi*	*qù*	*Zhōngguó.*
Lit.	He	not	go	China.

(He didn't go to China.)

word order

Word order in Chinese is not too different from English. The common patterns are:

subject + verb + object

Wǒ	*mǎi*	*dìtú.*
I	buy	map(s)

subject + specific time + verb + object

Tā	*liù diǎn*	*chī*	*wǎnfàn.*
He/She	six o'clock	eat	dinner

subject + verb + a period of time + object

Tā	*kàn le*	*yī ge xiǎoshí*	*diànshì.*
He/She	watched	an hour	TV

subject + place + verb (+ object)

Wǒ	*zài yínháng*	*gōngzuò.*
I	in a bank	work

questions

There are two ways to form questions requiring 'Yes' or 'No' answers:

● add the question word *ma* to the end of a sentence:

Tā shì Zhōngguórén.   He/She is Chinese.
Tā shì Zhōngguórén ma?   Is he/she Chinese?

● use the pattern: verb + negation word (*bù* or *méi*) + the same verb:

	Tā	*shì*	*bú*	*shì*	*Zhōngguórén?*
Lit.	He/She	be	not	be	Chinese
	(Is he/she Chinese?)				

Language **Builder**

When you ask a specific question using 'what', 'when', 'where', 'how', the sentence order is the same as that of a statement:

	Nǐ	*jiào*	*shénme?*
Lit.	you	are called	what

What's your name?

	Nǐ	*qù*	*nǎr?*
Lit.	you	go	where

Where are you going?

	Nǐ	*shénme shíhòu*	*qù*	*Zhōngguó?*
Lit.	you	when	go	China

When are you going to China?

	Nǐ	*zěnme*	*qù*	*Zhōngguó?*
Lit.	you	how	go	China

How are you going to go to China?

	Nǐ	*zài Zhōngguó*	*dāi*	*duō jiǔ/duō cháng shíjiān?*
Lit.	you	in China	stay	how long

How long are you going to stay in China?

	Nǐ	*yǒu*	*jǐ ge*	*Zhōngguó*	*péngyou?*
Lit.	You	have	how many	China	friend

How many Chinese friends have you got?

Using the question word *jǐ*, means the person asking the question expects a number less than 10 in the reply:

	Nǐmen bān	*yǒu*	*duō shǎo xuéshēng?*
Lit.	You class	have	how many students

How many students are there in your class?

By using the question word *duō shǎo*, the person who asks the question expects a number greater than 10 in the reply.

yes and no

The Chinese equivalents for 'yes' and 'no' are *shìde* and *bú shì*, but they are not used as extensively as in English. They are mainly used to answer questions that use *shì*:

Tā shì Zhōngguórén ma?	Is he/she Chinese?
Shìde./Bú shì.	Yes./No.

In English, standard answers to questions such as 'Do you like Chinese food?' are 'Yes, I do.' or 'No, I don't.' In Chinese you usually repeat the verb in the question in order to mean 'Yes.', and add the negative word before the verb when you want to say 'No.':

	Nǐ	*xǐhuān* *Zhōngguó fàn*	*ma?*
Lit.	You	like Chinese food	[question word]
	Do you like Chinese food?		

	Xǐhuān./Bù xǐhuān.
Lit.	Like./Not like.
	Yes, I do./No, I don't

Answers

Bare Necessities......

check out
1. Britain; yes, she has two children.
2. b
3. £100; £1 is at 15 kuai 3 mao

know-how
1 c 2 a 3 b

time flies ...
1 b 2 d 3 e 4 a 5 c

as if you were there
说一点儿。你从哪儿来？
shuō yìdiǎnr. nǐ cóng nǎr lái
你能说慢一点儿吗？
nǐ néng shuō màn yìdiǎnr ma
不是，我是美国人。
bú shì, wǒ shì měiguórén

Getting Around ....

check out
1. false
2. about 10 minutes; 30 kuai
3. b and c

matching
1 e 2 b 3 c 4 d 5 a

know-how
1 b 2 c 3 a 4 d

as if you were there
你好，买一张去长城的往返票。
nǐ hǎo, mǎi yī zhāng qù chángchéng de wǎngfǎn piào
有明天的票吗？
yǒu míngtiān de piào ma
一张。学生优惠吗？
yī zhāng, xuéshēng yōuhuì ma

Somewhere to Stay....

check out
1. a double room; 240 yuan a night
2. show your passport; 26
3. c; 150 yuan

match it up
1 e 2 d 3 c 4 b 5 a

mind the gap
1 b 2 d 3 a 4 c

as if you were there
请问，有空房间吗？
qǐng wèn, yǒu kòng fángjiān ma
一个双间，要两个单人床
yī ge shuāng jiān , yào liǎng ge dānrén chuáng
三个晚上，一个晚上多少钱？
sān ge wǎnshang, yī ge wǎnshang duō shǎo qián
可以看一下房间吗？
kěyǐ kàn yīxià fángjiān ma

Buying Things..........

check out
1 jasmine; half a jin
2 apples and bananas; 6 kuai
3 yes; too small

match it up
1 b 2 d 3 c 4 a

order, order
4, 3, 1, 2

as if you were there
我随便看看。
wǒ suíbiàn kànkan
我可以试试吗?
wǒ kěyǐ shìshi ma
有黑色的吗?
yǒu hēisè de ma

Eating out...............

check out
1 dumplings and hot pot; no monosodium glutamate
2 yes; coffee

match it up
1 b 2 a 3 a

menu mix-up
1 f, g, j
2 b, d
3 a, c, e, h, i

as if you were there
对不起,请结账。
duìbuqǐ, qǐng jiézhàng
我觉得这儿有个错。我们没有要啤酒。
wǒ juéde zhèr yǒu gè cuò. wǒmen méiyǒu yào píjiǔ
没关系。可以用信用卡吗?
méi guānxi. kěyǐ yòng xìnyòng kǎ ma

Entertainment..........

check out
1 c
2 Saturday evening; two and a half hours
3 yes; 200 kuai

question time
1 b 2 a 3 d 4 c

match it up
1 b 2 a 3 c

as if you were there
这儿有什么可看的?
zhèr yǒu shénme kěkàn de
我非常喜欢京剧。
wǒ fēicháng xǐhuān jīngjù
在哪儿买票?
zài nǎr mǎi piào
买三张票。
mǎi sān zhāng piào

Emergencies............

check out
1 true
2 cough mixture; take before meals
3 handbag; black; passport and a mobile phone

picture this
1 c 2 d 3 a 4 b

what do you need?
a 2, 5, 7
b 6, 8, 9
c 1, 3, 4

as if you were there
我感冒了。
wǒ gǎnmào le
我想试试中药。
wǒ xiǎng shishi zhōng yào
这种药怎么吃?
zhè zhǒng yào zěnme chī

A

a, an 一个 *yīge*
above 在..... 上 *zài...shàng*
accident 事故 *shìgù*
accommodation 住宿 *zhùsù*
across 穿过 *chuānguò*
acupuncture 针灸 *zhēnjiǔ*
adaptor 多路插座 *duōlù chāzuò*
address 地址 *dìzhǐ*
adult 成人 *chéngrén*
aeroplane 飞机 *fēijī*
again 再 *zài*
age 年龄 *niánlíng*
AIDS 艾滋病 *àizībìng*
air-conditioning 空调 *kōngtiáo*
airport bus 民航班车 *mínháng bānchē*
aisle 走道 *zǒudào*
alarm clock 闹钟 *nàozhōng*
alcohol 酒 *jiǔ*
all 所有的 *suǒyǒude*
allergic to 对... 过敏 *duì...guòmǐn*
alone 单独 *dāndú*
also 也 *yě*
altogether 一共 *yīgòng*
always 总是 *zǒngshì*
ambassador 大使 *dàshǐ*
ambulance 救护车 *jiùhù chē*
amount 数量 *shùliàng*
and 和 *hé*
angry 发怒 *fānù*
animal 动物 *dòngwù*
anniversary 周年 *zhōunián*
another 另一个 *lìngyīge*
appointment 约会 *yuēhuì*
architect 建筑师 *jiànzhùshī*
army 军队 *jūnduì*
around 周围 *zhōuwéi*
to arrange 安排 *ānpái*
arrival 到达/到站 *dàodá/dàozhàn*
art 艺术 *yìshù*
artist 艺术家 *yìshùjiā*
to ask 问 *wèn*
at 在 *zài*
athlete 运动员 *yùndòngyuán*
attractive 漂亮/迷人 *piàoliàng/mírén*

author 作家 *zuòjiā*
to be awake 醒了 *xǐng le*
away 出门了 *chūmén le*
awful 糟透了 *zāotòu le*

B

baby 婴儿 *yīng'ér*
back (reverse side) 反面 *fǎnmiàn*
bad 坏/糟糕 *huài/zāogāo*
bag 包 *bāo*
ball 球 *qiú*
ballpoint pen 圆珠笔 *yuánzhū bǐ*
bamboo 竹子 *zhúzi*
bank 银行 *yínháng*
bar 酒吧 *jiǔbā*
bath 洗澡 *xǐzǎo*
bathroom 卫生间 *wèishēng jiān*
battery 电池 *diànchí*
to be 是 *shì*
beautiful 美 *měi*
because 因为 *yīnwèi*
to become 当/成为 *dāng/chéngwéi*
bed 床 *chuáng*
before 从前;...前 *cóngqián; ... qián*
to begin 开始 *kāishǐ*
beginner 初学者 *chūxué zhě*
behind 后面 *hòumiàn*
Beijing (Peking) Opera 京剧 *jīngjù*
to believe 相信 *xiāngxìn*
below 在...下面 *zài... xiàmiàn*
belt 皮带 *pídài*
beside 在...旁边 *zài...pángbiān*
best 最好 *zuìhǎo*
better 更好 *gènghǎo*
better than... 比.... 好 *bǐ...hǎo*
between 在.... 之间 *zài...zhījiān*
beyond 在...以外 *zài...yǐwài*
bicycle 自行车 *zìxíngchē*
big 大 *dà*
bill 帐单 *zhàngdān*
bird 鸟 *niǎo*
birthday 生日 *shēngrì*
blanket 毯子 *tǎnzi*
to bleed 流血 *liúxiě*
blind (person) 盲人 *mángrén*
blonde 金发 *jīnfà*
blood 血 *xiě*

blood type 血型 *xiě xíng*
boarding gate 凳机口 *dēngjī kǒu*
boat 船 *chuán*
boiling water, boiled water 开水 *kāi shuǐ*
book 书 *shū*
to book 订 *dìng*
booking office 订票处 *dìngpiào chù*
boring 没意思 *méi yìsi*
to borrow 借 *jiè*
both 两; 都 *liǎng; dōu*
bottle 瓶子 *píngzi*
boy 男孩 *nánhái*
boyfriend 男朋友 *nán péngyou*
bra 胸罩 *xiōngzhào*
bracelet 手镯 *shǒuzhuó*
breakfast 早饭 *zǎofàn*
bride 新娘 *xīnniáng*
bridegroom 新郎 *xīnláng*
bridge 桥 *qiáo*
briefcase 手提箱 *shǒutí xiāng*
bright 亮/明亮 *liàng/míngliàng*
to bring 带来/带 *dàilái/dài*
brochure 说明书 *shuōmíngshū*
broken 断了; 摔坏了 *duàn le; shuāihuài le*
brother (younger) 弟弟 *dìdi*
  ›(elder) 哥哥 *gēge*
Buddhism 佛教 *fójiào*
Buddhist 佛教徒 *fójiàotú*
Buddhist temple 佛教寺院 *fójiào sìyuàn*
budget 预算 *yùsuàn*
buffet 自助餐 *zìzhùcān*
to build 建/盖 *jiàn/gài*
building 大楼 *dàlóu*
bus 公共汽车/巴士 *gōnggòng qìchē/ bāshì*
bus stop 公共汽车站 *gōnggòng qìchē zhàn*
to be on business 出差 *chūchāi*
business card 名片 *míngpiàn*
businessman/woman 商人 *shāngrén*
busy 忙 *máng*
to buy 买 *mǎi*

C

cabin 机舱 *jīcāng*
café 咖啡厅 *kāfēi tīng*
to call, to be called 叫 *jiào*
calligraphy 书法 *shūfǎ*
camera 照相机 *zhàoxiàngjī*
can (to be able to) 能/会 *néng/huì*
  ›(tin) 罐头 *guàntou*
to cancel 取消 *qǔ xiāo*
cancer 癌症 *áizhèng*
Cantonese (dialect) 广东话 *guǎngdōnghuà*
capital (city) 首都 *shǒudū*
car 车 *chē*
cards 卡片/牌 *kǎpiàn/pái*
career 职业/工作 *zhíyè/gōngzuò*
carriage (train) 车厢 *chēxiāng*
carrier bag 手提袋 *shǒutí dài*
cash 现金 *xiànjīn*
cashier 收款人 *shōukuǎnrén*
cat 猫 *māo*
to catch (thief) 抓 *zhuā*
  ›(train/bus) 赶 *gǎn*
CD 光盘 *guāngpán*
celebration 庆祝 *qìngzhù*
celebrity 名人 *míngrén*
centimetre 厘米 *límǐ*
centre 中心 *zhōngxīn*
century 世纪 *shìjì*
ceramics 陶瓷 *táocí*
certificate 证书 *zhèngshū*
change (coin) 零钱 *língqián*
to change (money/clothes) 换 *huàn*
changing room 更衣室 *gēngyī shì*
character (Chinese written character) 字 *zì*
charger (phone) 充电器 *chōngdiànqì*
cheap 便宜 *piányi*
to check in (at airport) 办理登机手续 *bànlǐ dēngjī shǒuxù*
  ›(at hotel) 办理住宿手续 *bànlǐ zhùsù shǒuxù*

to check out (at hotel)
办理离开手续 bànlǐ líkāi shǒuxù
Cheers! 干杯 gān bēi
chemist's 药店 yàodiàn
chess 象棋 xiàngqí
child, children 孩子, 小孩/儿童
háizi, xiǎohái/értóng
China 中国 zhōngguó
Chinese (language) 中文/汉语
zhōngwén/hànyǔ
»(people) 中国人 zhōngguórén
Chinese medicine 中药
zhōngyào
Chinese tea 中国茶 zhōngguó
chá
Chinese traditional medicine
doctor 中医 zhōngyī
to choose 挑/选 tiāo/xuǎn
chopsticks 筷子 kuàizi
Christian 基督教 jīdūjiào
Christmas 圣诞节 shèngdànjié
church 教堂 jiàotáng
cigarette 香烟 xiāngyān
cinema 电影院 diànyǐngyuàn
city 城市 chéngshì
classical 古典 gǔdiǎn
claustrophobia 幽闭恐怖症 yōubì
kǒngbù zhèng
clean 干净 gānjìng
clever 聪明 cōngmíng
client 客户 kèhù
cliff 悬崖 xuányá
climate 气候 qìhòu
to climb 爬 pá
clinic 诊所; 医务所 zhěnsuǒ;
yīwùsuǒ
cloakroom 存衣室 cúnyīshì
clock 钟 zhōng
to close 关 guān
clothes 衣服 yīfu
cloudy 多云 duōyún
coach (long distance bus) 长途
车 chángtúchē
coast 海边 hǎibiān
coat 大衣 dàyī
coat hanger 衣架 yíjià
coin 硬币 yìngbì
cold 冷 lěng

to have a cold 感冒 gǎnmào
colleague 同事 tóngshì
colour 颜色 yánsè
comb 梳子 shūzi
to come 来 lái
comfortable 舒服 shūfu
communism 共产主义 gòngchǎn
zhǔyì
company 公司 gōngsī
to complain; complaint 抱怨/埋怨
bàoyuàn/máiyuàn
complicated 复杂 fùzá
composer 作曲家 zuòqǔjiā
to compromise 让步 ràngbù
compulsory 必须的 bìxūde
computer 电脑/计算机 diànnǎo/
jìsuànjī
concert 音乐会 yīnyuèhuì
concert hall 音乐大厅 yīnyuè
dàtīng
condition 条件 tiáojiàn
condom 避孕套 bìyùntào
conference 会议/大会 huìyì/
dàhuì
to confirm 确认 quèrèn
Congratulations! 恭喜 gōngxǐ
connection 连接 liánjiē
conservation 保护 bǎohù
conservative 保守 bǎoshǒu
to consider 考虑 kǎolǜ
constipation 便秘 biàn mì
consulate 领事馆 lǐngshìguǎn
to contact 与... 联系 yǔ...liánxi
contact lens 隐形眼镜 yǐnxíng
yǎnjìng
to continue 继续 jìxù
contraceptive 避孕 bìyùn
contract 合同 hétong
to control 控制 kòngzhì
convenient 方便 fāngbiàn
conversation 对话/谈话 duìhuà/
tánhuà
to cook 做饭 zuò fàn
to cost 花 huā
cot 婴儿床 yīngér chuáng
cotton 纯棉 chúnmián
to cough 咳嗽 késòu
to count (number) 数 shǔ

country 国家 guójiā
countryside 农村 nóngcūn
couple (a pair) 一对儿 yīduìr
» (married) 夫妻 fūqī
credit card 信用卡 xìnyòng kǎ
crowd 一群人 yīqúnrén
crowded 拥挤/挤 yǒngjǐ/jǐ
cruise 游艇 yóutǐng
to cry 哭 kū
culture 文化 wénhuà
currency 货币 huòbì
customer 顾客 gùkè
to cut 切开/切 qiēkāi/qiē
cutlery 餐具 cānjù

D

daily 每天 měitiān
to damage 损坏/弄坏 sǔnhuài/
nònghuài
damp 潮湿 cháoshī
to dance 跳舞 tiàowǔ
dancer 舞蹈家 wǔdǎojiā
danger 危险 wēixiǎn
date 日期 rìqī
date of birth 出生日期 chū
shēng rìqī
daughter 女儿 nǚ'ér
day 天 tiān
dead 死 sǐ
deaf 聋 lóng
deep 深 shēn
to delay 推迟/延迟 tuīchí/yánchí
delicious 好吃/香 hǎochī/xiāng
to deliver 送 sòng
demonstration 游行 yóuxíng
dentist 牙医 yáyī
denture 假牙 jiǎyá
deodorant 腋下喷剂 yèxià pēnjì
to depart 离开 líkāi
department store 百货商店
bǎihuò shāngdiàn
departure (flight) 离港/离开
lígǎng/líkāi
» (train) 发车/开车 fāchē/
kāichē
deposit 押金 yājīn
to describe, description 描述
miáoshù
dessert 甜点 tiándiǎn

destination 目的地/终点
mùdìdì/zhōngdiǎn
detail 细节 xìjié
to develop (film) 冲洗 chōngxǐ
diabetes 糖尿病 tángniàobìng
to dial 拨号 bōhào
diamond 钻石 zuànshí
diarrhoea 拉肚子; 闹肚子 lā
dùzi; nào dùzi
dice 骰子 shǎizi
dictionary 字典/词典 zìdiǎn/
cídiǎn
to die 死 sǐ
difficult 难 nán
digital 数码 shùmǎ
dining room 餐厅 cāntīng
dinner 晚餐 wǎncān
diplomat 外交官 wàijiāoguān
direct 直接 zhíjiē
direction 方向 fāngxiàng
dirty 脏 zāng
disabled 残疾 cánjí
to disagree 不同意 bùtóngyì
disappointed 失望的 shīwàngde
disco 迪斯科 dísīkē
discount 打折 dǎzhé
dish (container) 碗 wǎn
» (food) 菜 cài
disposable 一次性 yícìxìng
distance 距离 jùlí
district 区 qū
to disturb 打扰 dǎrǎo
divorced 离婚了 líhūnle
dizzy 晕 yūn
to do 干/做 gàn/zuò
doctor 医生/大夫 yīshēng/dàifu
document 文件 wénjiàn
dog 狗 gǒu
dollar (Hong Kong) 港币
gǎngbì
» (US) 美元 měiyuán
domestic 国内 guónèi
door (train, car) 车门 chēmén
double 双 shuāng
double bed 双人床 shuāngrén
chuáng
double room 双人间 shuāngrén
jiān

down 下面 xiàmiàn
to download 下载 xiàzài
downstairs 楼下 lóuxià
draught (beer) 鲜啤酒/扎啤 xiānpíjiǔ/zhāpí
drink 饮料 yǐnliào
to drink 喝 hē
to drive 驾/开 jià/kāi
driving licence 驾驶执照 jiàshǐ zhízhào
to drown 淹死 yānsǐ
to drop 掉 diào
drunk 醉 zuì
dry 干 gān
dry cleaner's 干洗店 gānxǐ diàn
dubbed 配音的 pèiyīnde
during 在...期间 zài...qījiān
dusty 灰 huī
dynasty 朝代/朝 cháodài/cháo

E

each 每个 měige
early 早 zǎo
to earn 赚 zhuàn
earring 耳环 ěrhuán
earthquake 地震 dìzhèn
east 东 dōng
eastern 东方的 dōngfāngde
easy 容易 róngyì
to eat 吃 chī
economics 经济学 jīngjìxué
economy-class 经济舱 jīngjì-cāng
edible 可以吃的 kěyǐchīde
education 教育 jiàoyù
election 选举 xuǎnjǔ
electricity 电 diàn
email 电子邮件 diànzǐ yóujiàn
embarrassing 发窘/尴尬 fājiǒng/gān'gà
embassy 大使馆 dàshǐguǎn
emergency exit 紧急出口 jǐnjí chūkǒu
emperor 皇帝 huángdì
employee 雇员 gùyuán
employer 雇主 gùzhǔ
employment 就业 jiùyè
empress 女皇 nǚhuáng
empty 空 kōng

to end 结束 jiéshù
engaged (marriage) 订婚了 dìnghūnle
»(telephone) 占线 zhànxiàn
engineer 工程师 gōngchéngshī
English (language) 英语 yīngyǔ
to enjoy 享受; 喜欢 xiǎngshòu; xǐhuan
enough 足够 zúgòu
to enter 进入/进 jìnrù/jìn
entrance 进口/入口 jìnkǒu/rùkǒu
envelope 信封 xìnfēng
environment 环境 huánjìng
escalator 电梯 diàntī
Euro 欧元 ōuyuán
Europe 欧洲 ōuzhōu
even (number) 双 shuāng
evening 晚上 wǎnshang
event 事件 shìjiàn
every 每, 每个 měi, měige
every day 每天 měi tiān
everyone 每个人 měigerén
everywhere 每个地方, 到处 měige dìfang, dàochù
exactly 确实 quèshí
example: for example 比如 bǐ rú
excellent 优秀/出色 yōuxiù/chūsè
to exchange 交换 jiāohuàn
exchange rate 对换率 duìhuàn lǜ
excited, exciting 激动 jīdòng
excursion 郊游 jiāoyóu
excuse me 对不起/劳驾 duìbùqǐ/láojià
to exercise 锻炼 duànliàn
exhibition 展览 zhǎnlǎn
exit 出口 chūkǒu
expensive 贵 guì
to experience 经历 jīnglì
experienced 有经验的 yǒu jīngyànde
expert 专家 zhuānjiā
to explain, explanation 解释 jiěshì
explosion 爆炸 bàozhà
export, to export 出口 chūkǒu
express train 特快火车 tèkuài huǒchē
external 外部 wàibù

144

F

fabric 布料 *bùliào*
facilities 设施 *shèshī*
factory 工厂 *gōngchǎng*
to fail (exam, test) 没通过/没及格 *méi tōngguò/méi jígé*
failure 失败 *shībài*
to faint 晕倒 *yūndǎo*
fair (just) 公平 *gōngpíng*
fake 假的 *jiǎde*
false 假的 *jiǎde*
family 家庭 *jiātíng*
famous 有名/著名 *yǒumíng/zhùmíng*
fan (air) 扇子 *shànzi*
  »(supporter) 迷 *mí*
fantastic 太棒了 *tàibàngle*
far away 远 *yuǎn*
fare 票价 *piàojià*
farm 农场 *nóngchǎng*
farmer 农场主 *nóngchǎngzhǔ*
fashion 时装 *shízhuāng*
fashionable 时髦 *shímáo*
fast 快 *kuài*
fast food 快餐 *kuài cān*
father 父亲 *fùqīn*
fault 错误 *cuòwù*
favourite 喜爱的 *xǐàide*
fax 传真 *chuànzhēn*
fee 费 *fèi*
to feed 喂 *wèi*
female 女的 *nǚde*
festival 节日 *jiérì*
fever 发烧 *fāshāo*
fiancé 未婚夫 *wèihūnfū*
fiancée 未婚妻 *wèihūnqī*
fight 打架 *dǎjià*
file (document) 文件 *wénjiàn*
film (cinema) 电影 *diànyǐng*
finance 金融 *jīnróng*
to find 找 *zhǎo*
fine (penalty) 罚款 *fákuǎn*
fire 火 *huǒ*
fire extinguisher 灭火器 *mièhuǒ qì*
firework 焰火 *yànhuǒ*
first aid 急救 *jí jiù*
fish 鱼 *yú*

to go fishing 钓鱼 *diàoyú*
  fisherman 鱼民 *yúmín*
to fit 合适 *héshì*
  flash (for camera) 闪光灯 *shǎnguāngdēng*
  flat (apartment) 公寓/套房 *gōngyù/tàofáng*
  flavour 味道 *wèidào*
  flight 航班/飞机 *hángbān/fēijī*
  flood 洪水 *hóngshuǐ*
  floor (storey) 层 *céng*
  flour 面粉 *miànfěn*
  flower 花 *huā*
  fluent (language) 流利 *liúlì*
  fly (insect) 苍蝇 *cāngying*
to fly 飞 *fēi*
  food 饭 *fàn*
  food poisoning 食物中毒 *shíwù zhòngdú*
  football 足球 *zúqiú*
  for 为了 *wèile*
  Forbidden City 故宫/紫禁城 *gù gōng/zǐjìn chéng*
  foreign 外国的 *wàiguóde*
  foreigner 外国人 *wàiguórén*
  forest 森林 *sēnlín*
to forget 忘记 *wàngjì*
  fork 叉子 *chāzi*
  form (document) 表格 *biǎogé*
  formal 正式 *zhèngshì*
  fragile 虚弱 *xūruò*
  free (available) 有空 *yǒukòng*
  fresh 新鲜 *xīnxiān*
  friend 朋友 *péngyou*
  friendly 友好的 *yǒuhǎode*
  frightened 害怕 *hàipà*
  from 从 *cóng*
  front 前面 *qiánmiàn*
  fruit 水果 *shuǐguǒ*
  funeral 葬礼 *zànglǐ*
  funny 滑稽 *huájī*

G

  gallery 画廊 *huàláng*
  garden 花园 *huāyuán*
  garlic 大蒜 *dàsuàn*
  gate (at airport) 登机口 *dēngjīkǒu*
  »(entrance) 大门 *dàmén*

gentleman 绅士 *shēnshì*
to get off (the bus) 下 *xià*
to get on (the bus) 上 *shàng*
gift 礼物 *lǐwù*
ginger 生姜 *shēngjiāng*
girl 女孩 *nǚhái*
girlfriend 女朋友 *nǚ péngyou*
glass (material) 玻璃 *bōli*
»(for drinks) 玻璃杯 *bōlibēi*
glasses 眼镜 *yǎnjìng*
global warming 全球性变暖 *quánqiúxìng biànnuǎn*
to go 去 *qù*
God 上帝 *shàngdì*
gold 金子 *jīnzi*
gold-plated 镀金 *dù jīn*
golf 高儿夫 *gāo'ěrfū*
»golf course 高尔夫球场 *gāo'ěrfū qiúchǎng*
good 好 *hǎo*
»good evening 晚上好 *wǎnshang hǎo*
»good morning 早上好 *zǎoshang hǎo*
»good night 晚安 *wǎn'ān*
goodbye 再见 *zàijiàn*
government 政府 *zhèngfǔ*
grandparents 祖父母, 外祖父母 *zǔfùmǔ, wài zǔfùmǔ*
Great Wall 长城 *cháng chéng*
greedy 贪婪 *tānlán*
group 小组/团 *xiǎo zǔ/tuán*
guest 客人 *kèrén*
guide: tourist guide 导游 *dǎoyóu*
guidebook 导游书 *dǎoyóu shū*
guilty 内疚 *nèijiù*
gymnastics 体操 *tǐcāo*

H

hair 头发 *tóufa*
hairdresser's 发廊 *fàláng*
hair dryer 吹风机 *chuī fēngjī*
handbag 手提包 *shǒutíbāo*
handicapped 残疾人 *cánjírén*
handkerchief 手绢 *shǒujuàn*
handmade 手工做的 *shǒugōng zuòde*
to hang up 挂起来 *guà qǐlái*

hangover 宿醉/酒后头痛等 *sù zuì/jiǔhòu tóutòng děng*
happy 高兴 *gāoxing*
hard (not soft) 硬 *yìng*
»(difficult) 难 *nán*
he 他 *tā*
headache 头疼 *tóuténg*
headphones 耳机 *ěrjī*
heart attack 心肌梗塞 *xīnjī gěngsè*
heat 热气 *rèqì*
heating 暖气 *nuǎnqì*
heavy 重 *zhòng*
hello 你好 *nǐ hǎo*
to help 帮助 *bāngzhù*
Help! 救命 *jiùmìng*
here 这儿 *zhèr*
high 高 *gāo*
HIV 艾滋病毒 *àizī bìngdú*
»HIV positive 艾滋病毒阳性 *àizī bìngdú yángxìng*
hobby 爱好 *àihào*
holiday 度假/假期 *dùjià/jiàqī*
home 家 *jiā*
homosexual 同性恋 *tóngxìngliàn*
honest 正直的, 说实话 *zhèngzhide, shuō shíhuà*
honeymoon 蜜月 *miyuè*
Hong Kong 香港 *xiāng gǎng*
horse 马 *mǎ*
hospital 医院 *yīyuàn*
hospitality 好客 *hàokè*
host 主人 *zhǔrén*
hostess 女主人 *nǚ zhǔrén*
hot (spicy) 辣 *là*
»(for food and drinks) 烫 *tàng*
»(weather) 热 *rè*
hotel 饭店/宾馆 *fàndiàn/bīnguǎn*
hour 小时 *xiǎoshí*
how 怎么 *zěnme*
How far? 多远 *duō yuǎn*
How long? 多久 *duō jiǔ*
How many? (small number) 几 *jǐ*
»(large number) 多少 *duō shǎo*
How much? 多少钱 *duō shǎo qián*
How old? 多大了 *duō dà le*
humid 潮湿 *cháoshī*

to be hungry 饿 *è*
to hurt 疼 *téng*
  husband 丈夫/先生 *zhàngfu/ xiānshēng*

I

  I 我 *wǒ*
  ice 冰 *bīng*
  ill 病了 *bìngle*
  illness 疾病 *jíbìng*
to import 进口 *jìnkǒu*
  important 重要 *zhòngyào*
  in 在 *zài*
to include, included 包括 *bāokuò*
  industry 工业 *gōngyè*
  infection 感染/发炎 *gǎnrǎn/ fāyán*
  informal 不正式, 随便 *búzhèngshì, suíbiàn*
  information 信息 *xìnxī*
  injection 打针 *dǎzhēn*
to injure 受伤 *shòushāng*
  ink 墨水 *mòshuǐ*
  insect bite 虫子咬的 *chóngzi yǎode*
  insect repellent 驱虫剂 *qūchóng jì*
  inside 在...里面 *zài...lǐmiàn*
to insult 侮辱 *wǔrǔ*
  insurance 保险 *bǎoxiǎn*
  intelligent 聪明 *cōngmíng*
  interesting 有意思 *yǒuyìsi*
  international 国际 *guójì*
  Internet 互联网 *hùliánwǎng*
  Internet café 网吧 *wǎng bā*
  Internet connection 联网 *lián wǎng*
to interpret, interpreter 翻译 *fānyì*
  interval 间歇 *jiānxiē*
to introduce 介绍 *jièshào*
  iron 铁 *tiě*
  island 岛 *dǎo*
  ivory 象牙 *xiàngyá*

J

  jade 玉 *yù*
  jeans 牛仔裤 *niúzǎi kù*
  jeweller's 珠宝店 *zhūbǎo diàn*
  job 工作 *gōngzuò*

  joke 笑话 *xiàohua*
  journey 旅行, 路途 *lǚxíng, lùtú*
to jump 跳 *tiào*
  jumper 毛衣 *máoyī*

K

to keep 留下 *liúxià*
  key 钥匙 *yàoshi*
to kill 杀 *shā*
  kilogramme 公斤 *gōngjīn*
  kilometre 公里 *gōnglǐ*
to kiss 吻/亲吻 *wěn/qīnwěn*
  knife 刀 *dāo*
to knock 敲 *qiāo*
to know 知道 *zhīdào*
  knowledge 知识 *zhīshi*

L

  lake 湖 *hú*
  land 土地 *tǔdì*
  language 语言 *yǔyán*
  laptop 手提电脑 *shǒutí diànnǎo*
  large 大 *dà*
  late 晚 *wǎn*
  » be late 迟到 *chídào*
  later 后来 *hòulái*
  laugh 笑 *xiào*
  laundry 洗衣房 *xǐyīfáng*
  law 法律 *fǎlǜ*
  lawyer 律师 *lùshī*
to learn 学 *xué*
  leather 皮革 *pígé*
to leave 离开/走 *líkāi/zǒu*
  left 左 *zuǒ*
  left-luggage 行李寄存处 *xíngli jìcúnchù*
  length 长度/长短 *chángdù/ chángduǎn*
  lens (camera) 镜头 *jìngtóu*
  less 少 *shǎo*
  lesson 课 *kè*
  letter 信 *xìn*
  lift 电梯 *diàntī*
  light (not heavy) 轻 *qīng*
  » (colour) 浅 *qiǎn*
  lighter (cigarette) 打火机 *dǎhuǒjī*
to like 喜欢 *xǐhuān*
to listen 听 *tīng*

litter (rubbish) 废物 *fèiwù*
little 小 *xiǎo*
»a little 一点 *yīdiǎn*
to live 住 *zhù*
local 当地 *dāngdì*
to lock 锁 *suǒ*
long (length) 长 *cháng*
»(time) 久 *jiǔ*
to lose 丢失 *diūshī*
lost property 失物 *shī wù*
lot: a lot 很多 *hěn duō*
loud 大声地, 吵闹 *dàshēngde, chǎonào*
to love 爱 *ài*
luggage 行李 *xíngli*
lunch 午饭; 中饭 *wǔfàn; zhōngfàn*
luxury 豪华 *háohuá*

M

machine 机器 *jīqi*
magazine 杂志 *zázhì*
make-up 化妆品 *huàzhuāng pǐn*
male 男的 *nánde*
man 男人 *nánrén*
Mandarin 普通话 *pǔtōnghuà*
many 很多 *hěnduō*
map 地图 *dìtú*
market 自由市场 *zìyóu shìchǎng*
married 结婚了/已婚 *jiéhūnle/yǐhūn*
martial art 武术 *wǔ shù*
matches 火柴 *huǒchái*
mattress 垫子 *diànzi*
me 我 *wǒ*
meal 饭 *fàn*
meaning 意思 *yìsi*
meat 肉 *ròu*
mechanic 技师 *jìshī*
medicine 药 *yào*
medium 中等 *zhōngděng*
to meet 见面 *jiànmiàn*
»(somebody) 见; 见到 *jiàn; jiàndào*
meeting 会议 *huìyì*
memory stick 记忆棒 *jìyì bàng*
message 口信 *kǒuxìn*
metal 金属 *jīnshǔ*
meter (for taxi) 计程器 *jìchéngqì*
metre 米 *mǐ*

middle (size) 中等 *zhōngděng*
»(location) 中间 *zhōngjiān*
middle-aged 中年 *zhōng nián*
mile 英里 *yīnglǐ*
military 军事 *jūnshì*
milk 牛奶 *niúnǎi*
mineral water 矿泉水 *kuàngquán shuǐ*
minute (time) 分 *fēn*
minutes (of a meeting) 会议记录 *huìyì jìlù*
mirror 镜子 *jìngzi*
Miss 小姐 *xiǎojiě*
to miss (bus, train) 误了/没赶上 *wù le/méi gǎnshàng*
»(someone) 想 *xiǎng*
mistake 错误 *cuòwù*
mobile (phone) 手机 *shǒujī*
modem 调制解调器 *tiáozhì jiētiáoqì*
modern 现代 *xiàndài*
monastery 寺庙 *sìmiào*
money 钱 *qián*
Mongolia 蒙古 *ménggǔ*
monosodium glutamate 味精 *wèi jīng*
month 月 *yuè*
monument 纪念碑 *jìniànbēi*
more 多一点 *duōyīdiǎn*
morning 早上; 上午 *zǎoshang; shàngwǔ*
mosquito 蚊子 *wénzi*
mother 母亲 *mǔqīn*
motorbike 摩托车 *mótuōchē*
motorway 高速公路 *gāosù gōnglù*
mountain 山 *shān*
movie 电影 *diànyǐng*
museum 博物馆 *bówùguǎn*
music 音乐 *yīnyuè*
musician 音乐家 *yīnyuè jiā*
Muslim 穆斯林 *mùsīlín*

N

name 名字 *míngzi*
nappy: disposable 一次性尿布 *yícìxing niàobù*
national 全国的 *quánguóde*
nationality 国籍 *guójí*
natural 自然 *zìrán*

nausea 恶心 ěxīn
near, nearby 附近 fùjìn
necessary 必要 bìyào
to need 需要 xūyào
never 从来不 cóngláibù
new 新 xīn
news 新闻 xīnwén
newspaper 报纸 bàozhǐ
New Year 新年 xīn nián
 »Chinese New Year 春节 chūn jié
next 下 一个 xiàge yī
next to 旁边 pángbiān
nightclub 夜总会 yèzǒnghuì
no 不 bù
nobody 没人 méirén
noisy 吵闹 chāonào
non-alcoholic 不含酒精 bùhán jiǔjīng
normal 正常 zhèngcháng
north 北 běi
note (money) 纸币 zhǐbì
nothing 没什么 méishénme
now 现在 xiànzài
number 号码/号 hàomǎ; hào
nurse 护士 hùshi
nut 果仁 guǒrén

O

occupied 有人 yǒurén
o'clock 点; 点钟 diǎn; diǎnzhōng
official 官方的 guānfāngde
often 常常 chángcháng
okay 好的; 行 hǎode; xíng
old 老 lǎo
old-fashioned 老式; 过时 lǎo shì; guò shí
Olympic Games 奥林匹克运动会 àolínpīkè yùndòng huì
Olympic village 奥林匹克村 àolínpīkè cūn
on 在...上 zài...shàng
only 只有 zhǐyǒu
to open 打开 dǎkāi
opera 歌剧 gējù
 »Peking Opera 京剧 jīng jù
opposite 对面 duìmiàn
optician 眼镜店 yǎnjìng diàn
other 别的 biéde

our, ours 我们的 wǒmende
outdoors 露天 lùtiān
outside 外面 wàimiàn
owner 主人 zhǔrén

P

page 页 yè
pagoda 塔 tǎ
pain, painful 疼 téng
painting 画 huà
pair 对 duì
palace 宫殿 gōngdiàn
panda 熊猫 xióngmāo
paper 纸 zhǐ
parcel 包裹 bāoguǒ
pardon 对不起 duibuqǐ
parents 父母 fùmǔ
park 公园 gōngyuán
to park 停车 tíngchē
parliament 议会 yìhuì
party (political) 党 dǎng
 »(get-together) 聚会 jùhuì
to pass (a test) 及格 jígé
passport 护照 hùzhào
passport control 护照检查 hùzhào jiǎnchá
password 密码 mìmǎ
to pay 付/支付 fù/zhīfù
peace 和平 hépíng
pearl 珍珠 zhēnzhū
peanut 花生 huāshēng
pen 笔 bǐ
pencil 铅笔 qiānbǐ
penicillin 青霉素 qīngméisù
people, person 人 rén
P. R. China 中华人民共和国 zhōnghuá rénmín gònghé guó
perfume 香水 xiāngshuǐ
period (menstrual) 月经 yuèjīng
petrol 汽油 qìyóu
philosophy 哲学 zhéxué
photocopy 复印件 fùyìn jiàn
photograph 照片 zhàopiàn
phrase book 小词典, 手册 xiǎo cídiǎn, shǒu cè
pillow 枕头 zhěntóu
plane 飞机 fēijī
plasters 创可贴 chuàngkětiē

platform 站台 *zhàntái*
please 请 *qǐng*
plug (bath) 塞子 *sāizi*
  (electrical) 插头 *chātóu*
police, policeman 警察 *jǐngchá*
police station 警察局/公安局
jǐngchá jú/gōngān jú
pollution 污染 *wūrǎn*
pool (swimming) 游泳池
yóuyǒng chí
poor 穷 *qióng*
pop music 流行音乐 *liúxíng yīnyuè*
popular 受欢迎 *shòu huānyíng*
population 人口 *rénkǒu*
to post 寄 *jì*
postcard 明信片 *míngxìnpiàn*
post office 邮局 *yóujú*
to postpone 推迟/延期 *tuīchí/yánqī*
pound (sterling) 镑 *bàng*
pregnant 怀孕 *huáiyùn*
pretty 好看 *hǎokàn*
price 价格 *jiàgé*
priest 牧师 *mùshī*
prime minister 首相 *shǒu xiàng*
to print 印 *yìn*
prison 监狱 *jiānyù*
private 私人 *sīrén*
prize 奖品 *jiǎngpǐn*
problem 问题 *wèntí*
programme 节目 *jiémù*
to pronounce 念 *niàn*
pronunciation 发音 *fāyīn*
public 公共 *gōnggòng*
to pull 拉 *lā*
purse 钱包 *qiánbāo*
to push 推 *tuī*
to put on 穿 *chuān*

Q

quality 质量 *zhìliàng*
quay 码头 *mǎtóu*
queen 女王 *nǚwáng*
question 问题 *wèntí*
queue 队 *duì*
quick, quickly 快 *kuài*
quiet 安静 *ānjìng*

R

radio 收音机 *shōuyīnjī*
railway station 火车站 *huǒchē zhàn*
rain 雨 *yǔ*
to read 读/念 *dú/niàn*
receipt 收据 *shōujù*
reception (in hotel) 前台 *qiántái*
  (welcome party) 招待会
zhāodàihuì
refund 退款 *tuìkuǎn*
religion 宗教 *zōngjiào*
to remember 记得 *jìde*
remote 偏僻 *piānpì*
to remove 除去 *chúqù*
to repair 修 *xiū*
to repeat 重复 *chóngfù*
to reply 回答 *huídá*
reservation 预订 *yùdìng*
reserved 预订的 *yùdìngde*
restaurant 餐馆, 饭馆 *cānguǎn, fànguǎn*
retired 退休了 *tuìxiūle*
return ticket 往返票 *wǎngfǎnpiào*
rice wine 米酒 *mǐ jiǔ*
rich (person) 富, 有钱 *fù, yǒuqián*
to ride (bycicle) 骑 *qí*
right (not left) 右 *yòu*
  (correct) 对 *duì*
ripe (fruit) 熟 *shú*
river 河 *hé*
road 路 *lù*
room 房间 *fángjiān*
rude 粗鲁, 没礼貌 *cūlǔ, méi lǐmào*

S

sauce 汁, 酱 *zhī, jiàng*
scenery 风景 *fēngjǐng*
school 学校 *xuéxiào*
  primary school 小学 *xiǎo xué*
  secondary school 中学 *zhōng xué*
science 科学 *kēxué*
scissors 剪刀 *jiǎndāo*
sea 海 *hǎi*
seafood 海鲜 *hǎixiān*
seal (name stamp) 图章 *túzhāng*

seasick 晕船 *yūnchuán*
season 季节 *jìjié*
seat 座位 *zuòwèi*
to see 看见 *kànjiàn*
to sell 卖 *mài*
senior 高级 *gāojí*
separate 分开 *fēnkāi*
serviette 餐巾 *cānjīn*
sesame 芝麻 *zhīmá*
　»sesame oil 香油 *xiāng yóu*
to sew 缝 *féng*
sex 性 *xìng*
shampoo 洗发液 *xǐfàyè*
she 她 *tā*
shoe 鞋子 *xiézi*
shop 商店 *shāngdiàn*
shopping 买东西 *mǎidōngxi*
shopping centre 商业中心
shāngyè zhōngxīn
sick 生病, 呕吐 *shēngbìng, ǒutù*
sightseeing 观光 *guānguāng*
sign 标志 *biāozhì*
to sign, signature 签名; 签字
qiānmíng; qiānzì
silence, silent 沉默 *chénmò*
silk 丝绸 *sīchóu*
silver 银 *yín*
SIM card SIM 卡 *SIM kǎ*
to sing 唱歌 *chànggē*
Singapore 新加坡 *xīnjiāpō*
single (room) 单人 *dānrén*
　»(person) 单身 *dānshēn*
　»(ticket) 单程 *dānchéng*
sister (elder) 姐姐 *jiějie*
　»(younger) 妹妹 *mèimei*
to sit 坐 *zuò*
size 号码; 尺寸 *hàomǎ; chǐcùn*
to sleep 睡觉 *shuìjiào*
slow, slowly 慢 *màn*
small 小 *xiǎo*
smell 味儿 *wèir*
snow 雪 *xuě*
sometimes 有时候 *yǒushíhòu*
son 儿子 *érzi*
song 歌 *gē*
soon 马上 *mǎshàng*
sorry 对不起 *duìbuqǐ*
sour 酸 *suān*

south 南 *nán*
souvenir 纪念品 *jìniànpǐn*
to speak 说; 讲 *shuō; jiǎng*
speciality 专业 *zhuānyè*
to spend (money) 花 *huā*
　»(time) 过 *guò*
spicy 辣 *là*
sport 运动 *yùndòng*
stadium 室内体育馆 *shìnèi tǐyùguǎn*
stairs 楼梯 *lóutī*
stamps 邮票 *yóupiào*
to start 开始 *kāishǐ*
statue 塑像 *sùxiàng*
to stay 待; 住 *dāi; zhù*
to stop 停 *tíng*
street 街 *jiē*
student 学生 *xuéshēng*
subtitles 字幕 *zìmù*
sugar 糖 *táng*
suit 套装 *tàozhuāng*
suitcase 手提箱 *shǒutíxiāng*
sun 太阳 *tàiyáng*
sunburn 晒伤的皮肤 *shàishāng de pífū*
sunglasses 太阳眼镜 *tàiyáng yǎnjìng*
sunrise 日出 *rìchū*
supermarket 超级市场 *chāojí shìchǎng*
surname 姓 *xìng*
surprise 惊讶 *jīngyà*
to sweat 出汗 *chūhàn*
sweet 甜 *tián*
sweet and sour 糖醋 *táng cù*
sweetener 增甜剂 *zēngtiánjì*
sweets 水果糖 *shuǐguǒtáng*
to swim, swimming 游泳 *yóuyǒng*
swimming pool 游泳池 *yóuyǒng chí*
swimming trunks, swimsuit
游泳衣 *yóuyǒng yī*
swollen 肿了 *zhǒngle*

T

table 桌子 *zhuōzi*
table tennis 乒乓球 *pīngpāng qiú*

tailor 裁缝 *cáiféng*
to take 拿 *ná*
to take off 起飞 *qǐ fēi*
to take a photograph 照相; 拍照
zhào xiàng; pāi zhào
to talk 说话 *shuōhuà*
tall 高 *gāo*
tampons 月经棉塞 *yuèjīng miánsāi*
Taoism 道教 *dàojiào*
to taste 尝 *cháng*
tax 税收 *shuìshōu*
taxi 出租车 *chūzūchē*
tea 茶 *chá*
»tea house 茶馆 *chá guǎn*
teacher 老师; 教师 *lǎoshī; jiàoshī*
team 小组 *xiǎozǔ*
teapot 茶壶 *cháhú*
teenager 青少年 *qīngshàonián*
telephone 电话 *diànhuà*
to telephone 打电话 *dǎ diànhuà*
television 电视 *diànshì*
temperature 气温 *qìwēn*
»(fever) 发烧 *fāshāo*
temple 庙 *miào*
thanks, thank you 谢谢 *xièxie*
that 那, 那个 *nà, nàge*
theatre 剧院 *jùyuàn*
their, theirs 他们的 *tāmende*
them, they 他们 *tāmen*
then 然后 *ránhòu*
there 那儿 *nàr*
thousand 千 *qiān*
Tibet 西藏 *xīzàng*
ticket 票 *piào*
ticket office 售票处 *shòupiào chù*
time 时间 *shíjiān*
»what time is it? 几点了 *jǐ diǎn le*
timetable 时刻表 *shíkèbiǎo*
tired 累 *lèi*
tissues 面巾纸 *miànjīnzhǐ*
to have a toast 祝酒 *zhùjiǔ*
today 今天 *jīntiān*
toilet paper 卫生纸 *wèishēng zhǐ*
toilets 厕所 *cèsuǒ*
tomorrow 明天 *míngtiān*

tooth 牙 *yá*
»toothbrush 牙刷 *yáshuā*
»toothpaste 牙膏 *yágāo*
»toothpick 牙签 *yáqiān*
top (on top of) 在.....上头 *zài... shàng tou*
torch 电筒 *diàntǒng*
total 总数 *zǒngshù*
tourist 游客 *yóukè*
towel 毛巾 *máojīn*
tower 塔 *tǎ*
town 城 *chéng*
toy 玩具 *wánjù*
traffic 交通 *jiāotōng*
»traffic jam 交通堵塞 *jiāotōng dǔsè*
»traffic light 红绿灯 *hónglǜ dēng*
tram 电车 *diànchē*
train 火车 *huǒchē*
to translate, translator 翻译 *fānyì*
translation 翻译 *fānyì*
to travel 旅游 *lǚyóu*
travel agent 旅行社 *lǚxíng shè*
traveller's cheque 旅行支票 *lǚxíng zhīpiào*
travel sickness 晕车, 晕船, 晕机 *yūn chē, yūn chuán, yūn jī*
to turn 拐弯 *guǎiwān*
to turn off 关掉 *guān diào*

U

umbrella 雨伞 *yǔsǎn*
uncomfortable 不舒服 *bùshūfu*
under 在....底下 *zài....dǐxià*
underdone (meal) 不熟 *bùshú*
to understand 懂 *dǒng*
underwear 内衣 *nèiyī*
to undress 脱衣服 *tuō yīfu*
unemployed 失业 *shīyè*
uniform 制服 *zhìfú*
university 大学 *dàxué*
to unlock 打开 *dǎkāi*
until 直到 *zhídào*
up 上 *shàng*
urgent 急 *jí*
us 我们 *wǒmen*
USB lead U盘联线 *U pán liánxiàn*

V

valuables 贵重的 *guìzhòngde*
vegan 严格素食者 *yángé sùshízhě*
vegetables 蔬菜 *shūcài*
vegetarian 吃素 *chīsù*
vegetarian food 素菜;素食 *sù cài; sù shí*
vehicle 车辆 *chēliàng*
very 很 *hěn*
very much 十分 *shífēn*
view 景色 *jǐngsè*
village 村子 *cūnzi*
visa 签证 *qiānzhèng*
to visit 参观 *cānguān*
visitor 参观者 *cānguānzhě*
vitamin 维生素 *wéishēngsù*
voltage 电压 *diànyā*
to vomit 吐 *tù*

W

to wait 等 *děng*
waiter; waitress 服务员; 招待员 *fúwùyuán; zhāodàiyuán*
wallet 钱包 *qiánbāo*
watch 手表 *shǒubiāo*
to watch 看; 观看 *kàn; guānkàn*
water 水 *shuǐ*
waterfall 瀑布 *pùbù*
waterproof 防水 *fángshuǐ*
way out 出口 *chūkǒu*
we 我们 *wǒmen*
wealthy 富 *fù*
to wear 穿 *chuān*
weather 天气 *tiānqì*
weather forecast 天气预报 *tiānqì yùbào*
wedding 婚礼 *hūnlǐ*
week 星期 *xīngqī*
west 西 *xī*
western 西方的 *xīfāngde*
western food 西餐 *xī cān*
western-style 西式 *xī shì*
wet 湿 *shī*
what? 什么 *shénme*
wheelchair 轮椅 *lúnyǐ*
when? 什么时候 *shénme shíhòu*
where? 哪儿 *nǎr*
which? 哪个 *nǎge*

who? 谁 *shéi*
why? 为什么 *wéishénme*
wide 宽 *kuān*
wife 妻子; 太太; 夫人 *qīzi; tàitai; fūrén*
to win 赢 *yíng*
wind 风 *fēng*
windy 刮风了 *guāfēngle*
with 和, 跟 *hé, gēn*
without 没有 *méiyǒu*
woman, women 女的; 女人 *nǚde; nǚrén*
word 词 *cí*
world 世界 *shìjiè*
to write 写 *xiě*

X

X-ray X-光 *X-guāng*

Y

Yangtze River 长江 *cháng jiāng*
year 年 *nián*
Yellow River 黄河 *huáng hé*
yes 是的 *shìde*
yesterday 昨天 *zuótiān*
you (singular) 你 *nǐ*
 (plural) 你们 *nǐmen*
young 年轻 *niánqīng*
yuan (Chinese currency) 元 *yuán*

Z

zero 零 *líng*
zip 拉链 *lāliàn*
zoo 动物园 *dòngwùyuán*
zoom lens 可变焦距镜头 *kěbiàn jiāojù jìngtóu*

A

àihào 爱好 hobby
àiren 爱人 spouse
áizhèng 癌症 cancer
àizī bìngdú yángxìng 艾滋病毒阳
àizìbìng 艾滋病 AIDS
ānquán 安全 safe, safety
ānquán dài 安全带 seat belt
ānquán jiǎnchá 安全检查
security check

B

bàgōng 罢工 strike
bǎi 百 hundred
bànge 半个 half (n)
bāngzhù 帮助 to help
bànlǐ dēngjī shǒuxù 办理登机手续
to check in (at airport)
bànlǐ líkāi shǒuxù 办理离开手续
to check out (at hotel)
bāo 包 bag
bǎobèir 宝贝儿 darling,
sweetheart
bǎoxiǎn 保险 insurance
bēibāo 背包 rucksack
biǎogé 表格 form (document)
bìngle 病了 ill
bú kèqi 不客气 welcome:
you're welcome
bù yǔnxǔde 不允许的 forbidden
búliào 布料 fabric
bùshūfu 不舒服 uncomfortable
bùtóngyì 不同意 to disagree
bùzhèngshì 不正式 informal

C

cài 菜 dish (food)
cáiféng 裁缝 tailor
cānguǎn 餐馆 restaurant
cānguān 参观 to visit
cánjí 残疾 disabled
cānjù 餐具 cutlery
cǎoyào 草药 herb
cèsuǒ 厕所 toilets, lavatory
chá 茶 tea
cháng 尝 to taste
cháng chéng 长城 Great Wall
cháng jiāng 长江 Yangtze River
chángtúchē 长途车 coach

chǎo 炒 to stir-fry
cháodài 朝代 dynasty
chāojí shìchǎng 超级市场
supermarket
cháoxiǎn 朝鲜 Korea
chē 车 car
chéng 城 town
chéngrén 成人 adult
chéngshì 城市 city
chéngwéi 成为 to become
chēxiāng 车厢 carriage (train)
chēzhàn 车站 station
chī 吃 to eat
chǐcùn 尺寸 size
chīsù 吃素 vegetarian

chōuyān 抽烟 to smoke,
smoking
chuáng 床 bed
chuáng dān 床单 bed sheet,
linen
chuānghù 窗户 window
chuānglián 窗帘 curtain
chuántǒng 传统 tradition,
traditional
chuánzhēn 传真 fax
chūchāi 出差 to be on a
business trip
chūkǒu 出口 exit, export, to
export
chūxué zhě 初学者 beginner
chūzūchē 出租车 taxi
cí 词 word
cídiǎn 词典 dictionary
cìpǐn 次品 faulty
cūlǔ 粗鲁 rude, rough
(behaviour)
cúnyīshì 存衣室 cloakroom
cūnzi 村子 village
cuòwù 错误 error, mistake

D

dà 大 large, big
dà diànhuà 打电话 to telephone
dáfù 答复 answer
dǎhuǒjī 打火机 lighter
(cigarette)
dàifu 大夫 doctor

dàlóu 大楼 building
dàmén 大门 gate, entrance
dāngxīn 当心 careful, caution
dàojiào 道教 Taoism
dàshǐguǎn 大使馆 embassy
dàxué 大学 university
dǎzhé 打折 discount
diànhuà 电话 telephone
diànhuà kǎ 电话卡 telephone card
diànnǎo 电脑 computer
diànshì 电视 TV
diàntī 电梯 escalator, lift
diànyǐngyuàn 电影院 cinema
diànzǐ yóujiàn 电子邮件 email
dìngpiào chù 订票处 booking office
dìzhèn 地震 earthquake
dǒng 懂 to understand
dōng 东 east
dōngfāngde 东方的 eastern
dǒngshì huì 董事会 board of directors
dòngwù 动物 animal
dòngwùyuán 动物园 zoo
dǔbó 赌博 gambling
duì 对 correct
duì huàn lǜ 兑换率 exchange rate
duìbuqǐ 对不起 excuse me, sorry
dùjià 度假 holiday
duō dà le 多大了 how old?
duōméitǐ guāngpán 多媒体光盘 CD-Rom

E

è 饿 to be hungry
é'guó 俄国 Russia
ěrjī 耳机 headphones
értóng 儿童 children

F

fā diànzǐ yóujiàn 发电子邮件 to email
fāchē 发车 to depart (train/bus)
fákuǎn 罚款 fine (penalty)
fǎlǜ 法律 law
fàn 饭 food
fàndiàn 饭店 hotel
fànguǎn 饭馆 restaurant

fānù 发怒 angry
fānyì 翻译 to translate, translation
fāyán 发炎 infection
fēijīchǎng 飞机场 airport
fèiwù 废物 litter (rubbish)
fénmù 坟墓 grave (cemetery)
fěnsī 粉丝 fan (supporter)
fó 佛 Buddha
fójiào 佛教 Buddhism
fójiào sìyuàn 佛教寺院 Buddhist temple
fójiàotú 佛教徒 Buddhist
fù 富 wealthy
fūqī 夫妻 married couple
fùyǒu 富有 rich
fùzá 复杂 complicated

G

gān bēi 干杯 Cheers!
gǎngbì 港币 Hong Kong dollar
gānjìng 干净 clean
gāo'ěrfū 高尔夫 golf
gāojí 高级 senior, advanced
gāoxìng 高兴 happy
gē 歌 song
gēngyī shì 更衣室 changing room
gòngchǎn zhǔyì 共产主义 communism
gōngchǎng 工厂 factory
gōnggòng qìchē 公共汽车 bus
gōnggòng qìchē zhàn 公共汽车站 bus stop
gōngsī 公司 firm, company
gōngsī zǒngcái 公司总裁 CEO
gōngxǐ 恭喜 Congratulations!
gōngzī 工资 wage, salary
gōngzuò 工作 to work, job
guǎngdōnghuà 广东话 Cantonese
guāngpán 光盘 CD
guì 贵 expensive
gùkè 顾客 customer
guójì 国际 international
guójiā 国家 country
guónèi 国内 domestic
gùyuán 雇员 employee
gùzhǔ 雇主 employer

H

hǎi 海 sea
hǎicǎo 海草 seaweed
hǎixiān 海鲜 seafood
hángkōng gōngsī 航空公司 airline
hànyǔ 汉语 Chinese (language)
hǎochī 好吃 delicious
hǎohāo wánr 好好玩儿 fun: to have fun
háohuá 豪华 luxury
hǎojíle 好极了 wonderful, superb
hàokè 好客 hospitality
hé 河 river
hē 喝 to drink
hěnshǎo 很少 tiny (quantity)
hěnxiǎo 很小 (size)
hétóng 合同 contract
hóngshuǐ 洪水 flood
huángdì 皇帝 emperor
huánjìng 环境 environment
huānyíng 欢迎 to welcome
huāyuán 花园 garden
huìyì 会议 meeting, conference
hùliánwǎng 互联网 Internet
hūnlǐ 婚礼 wedding
huòbì 货币 currency
huǒchē 火车 train
huǒchē piào 火车票 train ticket

J

jí 急 urgent
jǐ 挤 crowded
jǐ 几 how many? (small number)
jǐ diǎn 几点 What time…?
jiāojuǎn 胶卷 film (for camera)
jiāoyóu 郊游 excursion
jiàoyù 教育 education
jiérì 节日 festival
jièshào 介绍 to introduce
jìjié 季节 season
jìn 近 nearby, not far
jīngjù 京剧 Beijing (Peking) Opera

jìngpiàn 镜片 lens, contact lenses
jǐngsè 景色 view
jīngshāng 经商 to do business
jìniànpǐn 纪念品 souvenir
jǐnjí chūkǒu 紧急出口 emergency exit
jìnkǒu 进口 import, to import, entrance
jīntiān 今天 today
jīntiān wǎnshang 今天晚上 tonight
jīntiān xiàwǔ 今天下午 this afternoon
jīntiān zǎoshang 今天早上 this morning
jùyuàn 剧院 theatre

K

kāfēi 咖啡 coffee
kāi shuǐ 开水 boiling/boiled water
kāichē 开车 to depart
kǎpiàn 卡片 cards
kě 渴 thirsty
kèrén 客人 guest
kēxué 科学 science
kēxuéjiā 科学家 scientist
kěyǐchīde 可以吃的 edible
kōng 空 empty
kòng fángjiān 空房间 vacancy (at hotel)
kōngtiáo 空调 air-conditioning
kǒuxiāng táng 口香糖 chewing gum
kòuzi 扣子 button
kǒuzi 口子 cut (wound)
kuài cān 快餐 fast food
kuàizi 筷子 chopsticks
kùzi 裤子 trousers

L

là 辣 spicy
làjiāo/làzi 辣椒/辣子 chilli
lāliàn 拉链 zip
láo jià 劳驾 excuse me
lǎoshī 老师 teacher
lěng 冷 cold
lìjí 立即 immediately

líkāi 离开 to leave, to depart
línshí 临时 temporary
líng 零 zero
língqián 零钱 change (coin)
língshìguǎn 领事馆 consulate
línyù 淋浴 shower (wash)
lìshǐ 历史 history
liúlì 流利 fluent (language)
lǐwù 礼物 gift
lìxí 利息 interest (bank)
lóushàng 楼上 upstairs
lóutī 楼梯 stairs
lóuxià 楼下 downstairs
lù 路 road
lúnyǐ 轮椅 wheelchair
lǔtú 路途 journey, trip
lùxiàn 路线 route
lǚxíng richéng 旅行日程 itinerary
lǚxíng shè 旅行社 travel agent
lǚyóu 旅游 to travel
lǚyóu chē 旅游车 tourist coach

M

mài 卖 to sell
mǎi 买 to buy
mài guāng 卖光 sold-out
mǎidōngxi 买东西 shopping
màn 慢 slow, slowly
máng 忙 busy
máojīn 毛巾 towel
máopí 毛皮 fur
měi 美 beautiful
měi, měige 每, 每个 every, each
méidiànle 没电了 flat (battery)
měige dìfāng 每个地方 everywhere
měigerén 每个人 everyone
měiguórén 美国人 American (people)
měitiān 每天 daily
měiyuán 美元 US dollar
měizhōu yícìde 每周一次的 weekly
mí 迷 fan (supporter)
mǐ jiǔ 米酒 rice wine
miǎn fèi 免费 free of charge
miào 庙 temple
mǐfàn 米饭 rice
míngpiàn 名片 business card

miyuè 蜜月 honeymoon
mòshuǐ 墨水 ink
mùtàn 木炭 charcoal
mùtou 木头 wood

N

nàge 哪个 which?
nán 南 south
nán 难 hard, difficult
nán péngyou 男朋友 boyfriend
nàr 那儿 there
nǎr 哪儿 where?
nǐ hǎo 你好 hello
nián 年 year
niàn 念 to read
niánlíng 年龄 age
niánqīng 年轻 young
nǚ zhǔrén 女主人 hostess
nuǎnhuo 暖和 warm (weather)
nuǎnqì 暖气 radiator, heating
nǚcèsuǒ 女厕所 ladies
nǚde, nǚrén 女的, 女人 woman, women, female
nǚ'ér 女儿 daughter
nǚhái 女孩 girl
nǚhuáng 女皇 empress

O

ǒutù 呕吐 to vomit, be sick
ōuyuán 欧元 Euro
ōuzhōu 欧洲 Europe

P

pāi zhào 拍照 to take a photograph
piānpì 偏僻 remote
piányi 便宜 cheap
piào 票 ticket
piào fáng 票房 box office
pígé 皮革 leather
píngzi 瓶子 bottle
pùbù 瀑布 waterfall

Q

qí 骑 to ride (bycicle)
qiān 千 thousand
qiánbāo 钱包 wallet
qiǎng 抢 to rob
qiānmíng, qiānzì 签名, 签字 to sign, signature

qiántái 前台 reception (in hotel)

qiānzhèng 签证 visa

qiáo 桥 bridge

qíchē rén 骑车人 cyclist

qǐng 请 please

qǔ xiāo 取消 to cancel

quánshuǐ 泉水 fountain

R

rè 热 hot (weather)

rēng diào 扔掉 to throw away

rèqì 热气 heat

rìběn 日本 Japan

rìběnrén 日本人 Japanese (people)

rìcháng yǐnshí 日常饮食 diet

rìchéng 日程 schedule

rìchū 日出 sunrise

rìqī 日期 date

rìwén 日文 Japanese (language)

róngyì 容易 easy

ruǎn yǐnliào 软饮料 soft drinks

ruǎnjiàn 软件 software

rùchǎng 入场 admission (to a park)

rùkǒu 入口 entrance

S

shǎizi 骰子 dice

shāngdiàn 商店 shop

shāngrén 商人 businessman, businesswoman

shāngǔ 山谷 valley

shǎnguāngdēng 闪光灯 flash (for camera)

shàngxiàbān shíjiān 上下班时间 rush hour

shāngyè zhōngxīn 商业中心 shopping centre

shéi 谁 who?

shéide 谁的 whose?

shēngjiāng 生姜 ginger

shēngri 生日 birthday

shēngyì 生意 business

shénme 什么 what?

shénme shíhòu 什么时候 when

shēnshì 绅士 gentleman

shēntǐ 身体 health

shēnzi 身子 body

shī wù 失物 lost property

shìde 是的 yes

shìgù 事故 accident

shíkèbiǎo 时刻表 timetable

shīyè 失业 unemployed

shǒubiǎo 手表 watch

shǒudū 首都 capital (city)

shōufèi 收费 to charge (money)

shǒugōng zuòde 手工做的 handmade

shōujù 收据 receipt

shǒujuàn 手绢 handkerchief

shōukuǎnrén 收款人 cashier

shòupiào chù 售票处 ticket office

shǒutí dài 手提袋 carrier bag

shǒutí diànnǎo 手提电脑 laptop

shǒutí xínglǐ 手提行李 hand luggage

shǒutí xiāng 手提箱 briefcase, suitcase

shǒutíbāo 手提包 handbag

shǔ 数 to count

shūfǎ 书法 calligraphy

shuǐ 水 water

shuǐguǒ 水果 fruit

shuǐguǒtáng 水果糖 sweets

shuìshōu 税收 tax

shùmǎ 数码 digital

sǐ 死 to die, dead

sīchóu 丝绸 silk

sījī 司机 driver

sù cài/sù shí 素菜/素食 vegetarian food

sù zuì 宿醉 hangover

sùdù xiànzhì 速度限制 speed limit

T

tā 她 she

tā 他 he, him

tā 它 it

tāde 她的 her, hers

tāde 他的 his

tàitai 太太 Mrs, wife

tàiyáng 太阳 sun
tāmen 他们 they, them
tāmende 他们的 their, theirs
tān 摊 stall, stand
tǎng xià 躺下 to lie down
tángniàobìng 糖尿病 diabetes
tánhuà 谈话 conversation
tǎnzi 毯子 blanket
tào cān 套餐 set menu
táocí 陶瓷 ceramics
tiānqì 天气 weather
tíqián 提前 in advance
tūn 吞 to swallow
tuō yīfu 脱衣服 to undress
túzhāng 图章 seal (name stamp)

U

U pán liánxiàn U盘联线 USB lead

W

wàiguórén 外国人 foreigner
wàijiāo shìwù 外交事务 foreign affairs
wàijiāoguān 外交官 diplomat
wǎn 晚 late
wǎn 碗 bowl, dish
wǎn'ān 晚安 good night
wǎncān 晚餐 dinner
wǎngqiú 网球 tennis
wánjù 玩具 toy
wǎnshang 晚上 evening
wǎnshang hǎo 晚上好 good evening
wèidào 味道 taste, flavour
wèir 味儿 smell
wèihūnfū 未婚夫 fiancé
wèihūnqī 未婚妻 fiancée
wèishēng jiān 卫生间 bathroom
wèishēng zhǐ 卫生纸 toilet paper
wèishénme 为什么 why?
wēixiǎnde 危险的 dangerous
wénhuà 文化 culture
wénjiàn 文件 file, document
wǒ 我 I, me
wò shǒu 握手 to shake hands

X

xī 西 west
xī cān 西餐 western food
xī shì 西式 western-style
xǐ'àide 喜爱的 favourite
xià yǔ 下雨 to rain
xián 咸 salty
xiāng gǎng 香港 Hong Kong
xiǎng jiā 想家 to be homesick
xiàngqí 象棋 chess
xiàngyá 象牙 ivory
xiāngyān 香烟 cigarette
xiànjīn 现金 cash
xiānsheng 先生 sir, Mr, husband
xiàochuǎn 哮喘 asthma
xiǎofèi 小费 tip
xiǎohái 小孩 child, children
xiǎoshí 小时 hour
xiǎozǔ 小组 team, group
xiàwǔ 下午 afternoon
xiàxuě 下雪 to snow
xiàzài 下载 to download
xīdú zhě 吸毒者 drug addict
xiě 写 to write
xiě xíng 血型 blood type
xièxie 谢谢 thanks, thank you
xìn yòng kǎ 信用卡 credit card
xìng 姓 surname, family name
xíngli 行李 luggage, baggage
xīnjiāpō 新加坡 Singapore
xìnxi 信息 information
xīnxiān 新鲜 fresh
xǐyīfáng 洗衣房 laundry
xīyǒu 稀有 rare
xīzàng 西藏 Tibet
xǐzǎo 洗澡 bath
xuǎnjǔ 选举 election
xué 学 to learn
xuéshēng 学生 student
xuéwèi 学位 university degree
xuéxí 学习 to study
xuéxiào 学校 school
xuéyuàn 学院 college

Y

yángé sùshízhě 严格素食者 vegan
yànhuǒ 焰火 firework
yǎnjìng 眼镜 spectacles, glasses
yáqiān 牙签 toothpick
yín 银 silver
yīng'ér 婴儿 baby
yīngbàng 英镑 sterling

yìngbì 硬币 coin
yīnggélán 英格兰 England
yīngguó 英国 Britain
yīngguórén 英国人 British (people)
yīngyǔ 英语 English (language)
yínháng 银行 bank
yǐnyòngshuǐ 饮用水 drinking water
yīnyuè dàtīng 音乐大厅 concert hall
yīnyuèhuì 音乐会 concert
yīqǐ 一起 together
yīqiè 一切 everything
yīqúnrén 一群人 crowd
yīshēng 医生 doctor
yìshù 艺术 art
yìshùjiā 艺术家 artist
yīyuàn 医院 hospital
yōngjǐ 拥挤 crowded
yǒuhǎode 友好的 friendly
yóukè 游客 tourist
yǒumíng 有名 famous
yóupiào 邮票 stamps
yǒuxiào 有效 valid (ticket)
yóuxíng 游行 demonstration
yóuyǒng chí 游泳池 swimming pool
yù 玉 jade
yuán 元 yuan (Chinese currency)
yùdìng 预订 reservation, to reserve
yuēhuì 约会 appointment
yǔfǎ 语法 grammar
yùjīn 浴巾 bath towel
yùnqìhǎo 运气好 lucky

Z

zàijiàn 再见 goodbye
zǎo 早 early
zǎofàn 早饭 breakfast
zǎoshang hǎo 早上好 good morning
zhāodàihuì 招待会 reception (welcome party)
zhàoxiàngjī 照相机 camera

zhē 蜇 to sting
zhè shìhé nǐ 这适合你 it suits you
zhèr 这儿 here
zhèngfǔ 政府 government
zhèngshi 正式 formal
zhèngshū 证书 certificate
zhēnjiǔ 针灸 acupuncture
zhòng 重 heavy
zhōngdiǎn 终点 destination
zhōngguó 中国 China
zhōngguórén 中国人 Chinese (people)
zhōngwén 中文 Chinese (language)
zhōng yào 中药 Chinese medicine
zhōng yī 中医 traditional Chinese medicine doctor
zhōumò 周末 weekend
zhōunián 周年 anniversary
zhùjiǔ 祝酒 to have a toast
zhǔrén 主人 host
zhùsù 住宿 accommodation
zhúzi 竹子 bamboo
zhùzuǐ 住嘴 Shut up!
zì 字 Chinese character
zì zhù 自助 self-service
zǐcài 紫菜 seaweed (edible)
zìdiǎn 字典 dictionary
zǒngbù 总部 headquarters
zōngjiào 宗教 religion
zǒngshì 总是 always
zǒngshù 总数 total
zuì 醉 drunk
zuòjiā 作家 writer, author
zuòqǔjiā 作曲家 composer
zuótiān 昨天 yesterday
zuòwèi 座位 seat
zuǒyòu 左右 about, approximately
zúqiú 足球 football, soccer